# Decent work
in
Denmark

International
Labour Office

# Decent work
# in
# Denmark

Employment,
social efficiency
and economic
security

Edited by Philippe Egger and Werner Sengenberger
in collaboration with Peter Auer, Marco Simoni and Corinne Vargha

Egger, P.; Sengenberger, W. (eds.)
*Decent work in Denmark: Employment, social efficiency and economic security*
Geneva, International Labour Office, 2003
Promotion of employment, labour market, labour policy, social policy, Denmark.
13.01.3

ISBN 92-2-113297-8

*ILO Cataloguing in Publication Data*

Typeset by Magheross Graphics, Switzerland & Ireland
Printed and bound in Great Britain by Biddles Ltd, *www.biddles.co.uk*

# FOREWORD

The central challenge facing the international community today is to make globalization work for the benefit of all. After over a decade of rapid expansion of global trade, and greater economic, technological and financial integration of the world's economies, many people and countries have clearly benefited from globalization. But many more have not, or have been disadvantaged. Expressions of anxiety, as well as of outright dissent, are found in many countries. These suggest that globalization is perceived as a threat to the security and values of people, without offering a solution to persistent poverty and social exclusion. Fundamental principles of equity and fairness, both within and between countries, have also received insufficient attention. These issues lie at the heart of the ILO mandate. That is why the goal of decent work – productive work in conditions of human dignity, freedom, equity and security for all women and men – has been adopted as the ILO's overarching objective. Decent work is now the framework for developing the ILO perspective and activities at both country and global levels.

The Working Party on the Social Dimension of Globalization of the ILO Governing Body, combining the views and experiences of government, employer and worker representatives from 56 countries, has debated these issues since 1994. The Working Party has moved in two directions. First, it has enlisted the support of all ILO constituents and of the international community for basic principles and standards defining a more equitable and inclusive pattern of development. This is the sense of the Declaration on Fundamental Principles and Rights at Work, adopted in 1998, a universal set of labour and social rights. This in turn derived from the World Summit for Social Development, held in Copenhagen in 1995, which called for a better integration of economic and social policies to promote secure and sustainable livelihoods on the basis of full employment, basic rights at work, equality of opportunity for women and men, and extensive social policies.

Second, the Working Party has examined the experience of a number of countries that appear to have successfully integrated the global economy on the basis of balanced social and economic policies, with a view to drawing useful lessons.

Denmark is one such country, demonstrating that openness and extensive social protection, employment flexibility and income security, high labour force participation rates, gender equity and family-friendly policies can go together. Indeed, the present study shows that Denmark's high living and working standards are both cause and consequence of economic growth and social development.

Denmark illustrates the promises held by a careful consideration of the Copenhagen Declaration on Social Development and Programme of Action of the World Summit for Social Development. It has elaborated detailed economic and social policies that enabled it to move decisively towards full employment; it has achieved substantial progress towards equality of opportunity in the labour market; it has taken steps to reconcile work and family life and to improve security at the workplace; and it has reformed its social protection system and further strengthened social dialogue and participation of the social partners. These achievements have all resulted in greater economic strength and social cohesion.

This study pays particular attention to the integration of social and economic policies and to the role of social dialogue. It shows that openness to international trade can go together with extensive social protection, and better and more secure lives. The condition for this is balanced policies, and strong institutions, of government, the social partners and civil society.

Each country will need to define its own path towards decent work, building on the principles and standards universally shared by the ILO constituents. In so doing, each path can benefit from the experience of others. Inspiration and mutual learning from other national situations and practices are always enriching. This is valid across regions and levels of development, both for countries that have moved toward greater material ease in sustaining decent work, and those still struggling to ensure basic rights and minimal living standards.

The basic challenge of our times lies in providing people with the opportunities and the support required to secure and sustain decent work. In this, Denmark illustrates a way and offers some results that can usefully inspire others. This study is one example of the many ways in which the ILO works with its constituents in their commitment to promote decent work for all women and men.

*Juan Somavia*
*Director-General*
*International Labour Organization*

# CONTENTS

Foreword . . . . . . . . . . . . . . . . . . . . . . . . . . . . . . . . . . . . . . . . . . . . . . . . v

Preface . . . . . . . . . . . . . . . . . . . . . . . . . . . . . . . . . . . . . . . . . . . . . . . . . xi

Abbreviations and acronyms used in this book . . . . . . . . . . . . . . . . . . . . xiii

Introduction . . . . . . . . . . . . . . . . . . . . . . . . . . . . . . . . . . . . . . . . . . . . . 1

1   Working and living conditions in Denmark: The statistical indicators . . . 5

Indicators of decent work . . . . . . . . . . . . . . . . . . . . . . . . . . . . . . . . . . 6

   Labour force participation . . . . . . . . . . . . . . . . . . . . . . . . . . . . . . . . 6

   Employment . . . . . . . . . . . . . . . . . . . . . . . . . . . . . . . . . . . . . . . . . 6

   Part-time employment . . . . . . . . . . . . . . . . . . . . . . . . . . . . . . . . . . 7

   Fixed-term employment . . . . . . . . . . . . . . . . . . . . . . . . . . . . . . . . . 7

   Unemployment . . . . . . . . . . . . . . . . . . . . . . . . . . . . . . . . . . . . . . 8

   Inactivity . . . . . . . . . . . . . . . . . . . . . . . . . . . . . . . . . . . . . . . . . . 8

   Educational and vocational training . . . . . . . . . . . . . . . . . . . . . . . . . 9

   Working hours . . . . . . . . . . . . . . . . . . . . . . . . . . . . . . . . . . . . . . 10

   Level and growth of wages . . . . . . . . . . . . . . . . . . . . . . . . . . . . . . 10

   Wage and income distribution . . . . . . . . . . . . . . . . . . . . . . . . . . . . 11

   Occupational safety and health . . . . . . . . . . . . . . . . . . . . . . . . . . . 18

   Social protection and welfare . . . . . . . . . . . . . . . . . . . . . . . . . . . . 19

   Gender equality . . . . . . . . . . . . . . . . . . . . . . . . . . . . . . . . . . . . . 23

   Fundamental rights at work and international labour standards . . . . . . . . 27

   Collective organization, collective bargaining and collective action . . . . . . . 28

Indicators of economic performance ............................... 30

    Labour productivity ........................................... 30

    Prosperity ................................................... 30

    Economic growth ............................................. 31

    Inflation .................................................... 31

    Taxation .................................................... 31

    Fiscal and trade balance ...................................... 33

    Business environment and competitiveness ....................... 33

Progress and setbacks ............................................ 35

A summary assessment ........................................... 38

**2    How Denmark has attained decent work: Institutions and policies** ... 43

Basic institutional features ........................................ 43

Social and economic policies ...................................... 47

    Collective bargaining and social dialogue ......................... 47

    Occupational safety and health .................................. 54

    Social security and welfare ..................................... 56

    Gender equality .............................................. 62

    Labour market and training policies .............................. 65

    Interaction between microeconomic and macroeconomic policy .......... 75

    Flexible enterprises and flexible work organization ................... 80

The social foundations of decent work: A synthesis .................... 81

**3    Challenges** ................................................. 87

Maintaining welfare through adequate labour supply .................... 87

Sustaining flexicurity in the labour market .......................... 89

Achieving full employment ........................................ 90

Full employment and decent work ................................... 90

Labour market implications of an ageing workforce .................... 92

High growth in labour productivity ................................. 92

Taxation and labour supply ....................................... 93

Denmark in the European Union .................................... 94

Strong institutions and social dialogue ............................. 95

**Bibliography** ................................................. 97

# List of tables

1    Percentage distribution of full-time equivalent income
transfer recipients by type of benefit in Denmark, 1998 . . . . . . . . . . . . . . . . . 20

2    Percentage of women in different employment sectors in Denmark, 1999 . . . . . . 25

3    Comparison of core economic and social indicators in Denmark,
the United States, the EU and the OECD . . . . . . . . . . . . . . . . . . . . . . . . . . 34

4    Selected economic and social indicators, Denmark, 1913–92 . . . . . . . . . . . . . . . 37

5    Average annual percentage change in wages, productivity and
income in Denmark, Germany and Sweden, 1986–92 and 1993–99 . . . . . . . . 52

6    Change in real wages by economic activity in Denmark, 1996–98 . . . . . . . . . . . 52

7    Labour market policy expenditure and participant inflow in Denmark, 1997–2000 . 71

8    Decomposition of GDP per capita, 1998 US$ at PPP . . . . . . . . . . . . . . . . . . . . 75

9    Employment to working-age population ratios, 2000 . . . . . . . . . . . . . . . . . . . . . 76

# List of figures

1    Labour force participation rate, 2000 . . . . . . . . . . . . . . . . . . . . . . . . . . . . . . . . 12

2    Employment rate, 2000 . . . . . . . . . . . . . . . . . . . . . . . . . . . . . . . . . . . . . . . . . 12

3    Total part-time work as a percentage of total employment and
part-time work of women, 1990 and 2000 . . . . . . . . . . . . . . . . . . . . . . . . . . 13

4    Unemployment rates as percentage of the labour force, 2000 . . . . . . . . . . . . . . 14

5    Inactivity rate, 1999 . . . . . . . . . . . . . . . . . . . . . . . . . . . . . . . . . . . . . . . . . . . 15

6    Level of educational attainment in the labour force, 1998 . . . . . . . . . . . . . . . . . 15

7    Annual and weekly average working hours, 1998 and 1999 . . . . . . . . . . . . . . . . 16

8    Annual percentage change in real hourly earnings in manufacturing, 1989–99 . . . . 17

9    Relative shares of total income in Denmark and the European Union, 1996 . . . . 17

10   Total public social security expenditure as a percentage of GDP, mid-1990s . . . . 23

11   Labour force participation rate in Denmark, by sex, 1960–2000 . . . . . . . . . . . . 24

12   Proportion of women in different occupational groups in Denmark, 1998 . . . . . . 25

13   Female wages as a percentage of male wages in the private
and state sectors, Denmark, 1996 . . . . . . . . . . . . . . . . . . . . . . . . . . . . . . . . 26

14   Social dialogue in the mid-1990s . . . . . . . . . . . . . . . . . . . . . . . . . . . . . . . . . . 29

15   Tax revenue by main headings as a percentage of total taxation, 1998 . . . . . . . . 32

16   GDP per capita in Denmark, 1960–98 . . . . . . . . . . . . . . . . . . . . . . . . . . . . . . 36

17   Unemployment rate in Denmark, 1960–2000 . . . . . . . . . . . . . . . . . . . . . . . . . 38

18   Social expenditure rates in the United States and Denmark, 1997 . . . . . . . . . . . 59

19   The golden triangle of "flexicurity" . . . . . . . . . . . . . . . . . . . . . . . . . . . . . . . . 67

20   Unemployment rate as percentage of total labour force, 1970–2000 . . . . . . . . . 70

# PREFACE

Promoting opportunities for women and men to obtain decent and productive work in conditions of freedom, equity, security and human dignity is the overarching objective of the International Labour Organization (ILO). The International Labour Conference endorsed the Decent Work concept in 1999 and 2001 (ILO, 1999; 2001c). Decent work stems from the convergence of four strategic objectives, namely the promotion of rights at work; employment; social protection; and social dialogue. Decent work is simultaneously an objective for all ILO programmes and activities, and a central feature of the international development agenda. The central challenge is to turn the aspiration of working people in all countries for decent work into a reality.

In 1998–99, the ILO carried out a comparative review of employment policies in Austria, Denmark, Ireland and the Netherlands. This was a follow-up to Commitment Three concerning full employment and sustainable livelihoods, of the Copenhagen Declaration and Programme of Action, adopted at the World Summit for Social Development in 1995. The four small European economies were chosen because they had demonstrated over the 1990s a labour market performance far superior to the European Union average. While the specific policies and measures pursued in the respective countries varied, there were clearly a number of common institutional and policy elements to which their labour market success could be attributed. One of them concerned the prominent role played by social dialogue on employment and labour market policy issues between the governments and the social partners at the national level (Auer, 2000; 2001).

The employment policy reviews of the four European countries have received wide attention and met with considerable interest among the ILO constituencies in various parts of the world. They have contributed to raising interest in various countries in concluding social agreements in order to promote national employment goals.

In the meantime, the Danish Ministry of Labour requested the ILO to follow up the Danish employment policy review. The ILO responded by proposing to undertake a Decent Work Programme for Denmark. The Government and the social partners welcomed this proposal.

This exercise has provided an opportunity to extend and deepen the cooperation between the ILO and Denmark in policy areas that are of outstanding concern to both. The interest of the Danish partners lies in working with the ILO in addressing, in a comparative perspective, prevailing policy issues in Denmark, particularly as regards the labour market and social protection. The ILO's interest is in reaching a deeper understanding of the policies and practices in which Denmark has played a pioneering role and in which it may be seen as very advanced on a world scale. These include collective bargaining and social dialogue; the system of vocational education and training; the active labour market policy; the combination of labour market flexibility and income security; policies and instruments for reconciling work and family life; and the reform of social protection and welfare. All of these are central to the ILO's mandate and the subject of ILO normative instruments.

The report has been prepared by an ILO team comprising Peter Auer, Philippe Egger, Werner Sengenberger, Marco Simoni and Corinne Vargha. Responsibility for the content of the report rests fully with the ILO.

In preparing this report, the ILO greatly benefited from background information on relevant policies in Denmark provided by the Danish Government through the Ministry of Labour. Contributions have been received from the Ministry of Labour, the Ministry of Social Affairs, the Danish Employers' Confederation (DA) and the Danish Confederation of Trade Unions (LO). A series of consultations between the Danish constituents and the ILO team were held in Copenhagen and Geneva, which provided opportunities for detailed exchanges and discussions. The ILO acknowledges the support provided by its Danish counterparts and wishes to express its gratitude, especially to Joergen Eckersoth, Preben Foldberg, Anne Marie Jensen, Anne Mette Krabbe Skousen, Elisabeth Rasmussen, Joergen Roennest and Kim Taasby. Thanks are also due to several Danish academic experts, in particular Per Madsen, for information and advice.

# ABBREVIATIONS AND ACRONYMS USED IN THIS BOOK

| | |
|---|---|
| AC | Danish Confederation of Graduate Employee Associations |
| CEDEFOP | European Centre for the Development of Vocational Training |
| DA | Danish Employers' Confederation |
| ECB | European Central Bank |
| EEC | European Economic Community |
| EMU | European Monetary Union |
| ERM | exchange rate mechanism |
| EU | European Union |
| FTF | Confederation of White-Collar and Crown Servants |
| GDP | gross domestic product |
| ILO | International Labour Organization |
| ISCED | International Standard Classification of Education |
| ISCO | International Standard Classification of Occupations |
| LO | Danish Confederation of Trade Unions |
| OECD | Organisation for Economic Co-operation and Development |
| OSH | occupational safety and health |
| PPP | purchasing power parity |
| UNDP | United Nations Development Programme |
| VET | vocational education and training |

# INTRODUCTION

Decent work in Denmark is reflected in high levels of income, security, and social and gender equality, as well as in labour standards on rights to work and rights at work. This has been achieved through a combination of effective public policies implemented by national, regional and local institutions, dynamic private enterprises, extensive participation of workers and citizens directly and through representative bodies, and a high level of public social spending, as well as relatively high growth in total output and in gross domestic product (GDP) per capita. The policy choices made in Denmark have not opposed private and public sectors, economic growth and public social spending; rather they have aimed to build on their integration and complementarities. Particular care has been taken to ensure that the benefits of growth flow into comprehensive social security and welfare and, at the same time, that social expenditure does not stifle growth through declining investment, uncompetitive labour costs and unsustainable fiscal deficits. In this sense, Denmark's achievements run contrary to the conventional wisdom of the 1980s and early 1990s, when policy prescriptions aimed at combating European sclerosis suggested a reduction in welfare benefits, less government intervention and greater labour market flexibility as a basis for renewed growth. In fact, Denmark has moved onto a higher and so far sustained growth path since the early 1990s, significantly reducing unemployment much earlier than most other European countries. It has done so, not by turning its back on the traditional welfare model, but by adapting it to a new economic context in which high employment rates coexist with balanced fiscal budgets, a trade surplus, and low and stable inflation. In many ways, Denmark adapted the central features of the "Golden Age" (1950–73) to the new situation of the 1990s, which was marked in particular by the emergence of global product and capital markets (Singh, 1995). The period 1950–73 was characterized by rapid and parallel growth in real output, wages and productivity, institutional arrangements reflecting social consensus for the setting of wages and prices and the distribution of wages and profits, and fiscal and welfare policies that guaranteed rising living standards and sustained aggregate demand. Many features of that period can be observed in Denmark today within a totally distinct context. In particular, one prominent element of the Golden Age then, and of Denmark today, is the wage-coordinating mechanism that allows wages to be adjusted in line with the growth of the economy. These adjustments are perceived as fair and workable because of the extensive welfare benefits and policies that ensure progressive redistribution of income.

This book examines to what extent, and by what means and mechanisms, the high labour standards and relatively equal income distribution, facilitated by high employment rates and social protection, have contributed to sustaining a high rate of economic growth. As Denmark has a relatively open economy, growth is largely dependent on competitive exports and export-oriented enterprises. Likewise, it is of particular interest to learn how Denmark has succeeded in sustaining its competitiveness with high standards of labour and social protection. The conclusion is that such standards are not only a consequence of economic growth, but also an essential basis for growth and competitiveness.

In this respect, social protection and social dialogue have played a dynamic role in sustaining Denmark's decent work achievements. Social protection stimulates savings, sustains aggregate demand through more equal income distribution and, by cushioning business cycles, makes possible high employment rates, particularly of women, upholds high labour productivity, and facilitates technological, social and economic change by ensuring income and social security of workers and their families. At the same time, social dialogue on economic, social and labour policy choices ensures a high degree of coherence in policy-making in the face of competing demands on limited resources.

Denmark is of special interest in relation to the manner in which economic and social problems are confronted and solved. Of course, as in most other countries, there have been problems linked to global competition, business cycles, periods of higher than average unemployment, inflationary pressures and the high costs of social protection. Denmark was afflicted by such problems from the early 1970s to the early 1990s. By the late 1990s, however, the country had by and large managed to overcome them. New, innovative labour market policies were put in place. The welfare state was reformed and now seems more solidly entrenched than ever. It has proven resilient and viable in an era of rapidly advancing globalization that poses particular threats to small and open economies. Social dialogue and collective bargaining have undergone major changes while remaining true to their original principles, resulting in their greater strength.

The above remarks do not imply that all is well in Denmark. The Decent Work agenda is a dynamic one. First, sustaining the present levels is a challenge in itself, especially in a small open economy exposed to a volatile world market. Second, new challenges and new demands emerge continuously in all of the areas mentioned above. The ageing Danish population poses fundamental challenges to the labour market and the welfare system; new demands are placed on gender equality and on occupational safety and health, particularly in relation to high-intensity work; the effectiveness of active labour market policies is continually tested, as well as the ability of the social partners to respond to competing demands. Mention must also be made of global concerns such as sustainable development and the use of alternative non-fossil energy sources, in which Denmark is very active.

By looking at Denmark one can capture salient features of the employment policy debate within the European Union (EU). This policy seeks to create more and better jobs. The Treaty of Amsterdam and the Jobs Summit of 1997 in Luxembourg laid the basis of an agreement on a European Employment Strategy, with European-wide guidelines (on employability, entrepreneurship, adaptability and gender equality), and a national action planning process involving the monitoring of commonly defined quantified employment targets. They also underscored the role of the social partners in designing labour market policies that combine flexibility and security. In tandem with Europe's transition to a knowledge-based economy, the European Council meetings in Nice in 2000 and Stockholm in 2001 stressed the need to raise the quality of work throughout Europe. They called for improvements across several dimensions of quality in work: a good working environment for all; equal opportunities and gender equality; flexible work organization that allows for a better balance between work and personal life; lifelong learning; health and safety at work; and employee involvement and diversity at work. These concerns accord with the ILO's Decent Work paradigm. The European Commission has proposed to undertake periodic "quality reviews" to ensure that Member States' employment and social policies are designed to achieve the standards of the best performers. This report addresses these concerns and represents a contribution to wider EU/ILO collaboration in promoting policies and action for decent work for all women and men.

# WORKING AND LIVING CONDITIONS IN DENMARK: THE STATISTICAL INDICATORS

# 1

This chapter provides a statistical portrait of Denmark. Social and economic indicators for Denmark are assessed and compared with those of other industrialized countries. In so far as the availability and comparability of data allow, one or several countries performing best on each of the indicators are taken as the reference, together with the 15 member countries of the European Union (EU-15), 20 member countries of the Organisation for Economic Co-operation and Development (OECD), and the United States (being the largest OECD member country). This benchmarking illustrates where Denmark stands, in absolute and relative terms, with regard to the strategic objectives of decent work, including basic worker rights and international labour standards, employment and income, social protection and social dialogue. For each indicator, the most recent data available are used.

The statistical information used in this report comes from various sources, including the Bureau of Labour Statistics of the United States Government, Eurostat and the European Commission, the European Foundation for the Improvement of Living and Working Conditions, the ILO, OECD, and Statistics Denmark, all of which collect and process data from primary national sources.

Unless otherwise indicated, the figures concerning the OECD-20 group refer to the unweighted average of the industrialized OECD countries, barring Luxembourg and Iceland. These two countries were omitted because of their small size and because for many indicators they are outliers in the distribution of values. The 20 OECD countries are: Australia, Austria, Belgium, Canada, Denmark, Finland, France, Germany, Greece, Ireland, Italy, Japan, Netherlands, New Zealand, Norway, Portugal, Spain, Sweden, the United Kingdom and the United States.

# Indicators of decent work

## Labour force participation

In 2000, four-fifths of the Danish population of working age were in the labour force. The **labour force participation rate** was exactly 80.0 per cent of the population aged 15–64 years, (see figure 1 on page 12). This was higher than the rate for the United States (77.2 per cent), and 10.5 percentage points above the mean rate for the EU-15. The rate for women in Denmark was 75.9 per cent, which was the second highest EU figure after Sweden (which registered 76.4 per cent for its population aged 16 to 64 years) (OECD, 2001a).

## Employment

More than three-quarters of Danes of working age are employed. In 2000, the **employment to population ratio (or employment rate)**, i.e. the proportion of the population aged between 15 and 64 years who were employed, was 76.4 per cent. Since 1994, this rate has risen by 3.7 percentage points. Denmark's employment rate is by far the highest among the member countries of the European Union. It is nearly 13 percentage points above the EU-15 average rate of 63.6 per cent. Moreover, Denmark had the second-highest level of employment in the OECD-20, only Norway's being higher at 77.8 per cent (population aged 16–64 years). Sweden and the United States followed with 74.2 per cent and 74.1 per cent, respectively.

The **employment rate for men** was 80.7 per cent in 2000, **the employment rate for women** 72.1 per cent (see figure 2 on page 12). Only in Norway and Sweden (74.0 and 72.3 per cent respectively, population aged 16–64 years) was a higher proportion of women employed than in Denmark. The average employment rate for women for the EU-15 group was 53.9 per cent, that is 18.2 percentage points below the Danish rate.

Denmark already substantially exceeds the target employment rates set for 2010 by the European Council at its Summit Meeting in Lisbon in 2000 (an overall employment rate of 70 per cent, and for women of 60 per cent).

The **employment rate for young people** in the age group 15–24 years was 67.1 per cent. Again, this is the second-highest rate among the industrialized countries after the Netherlands, where the figure for 2000 reached 68.4 per cent. It compares with an average of 40.8 per cent for the EU, and 47.4 per cent among the OECD-20 countries. An even greater difference is found in the employment rate of young women: 64.0 per cent in Denmark and an average of 36.7 per cent in the EU (OECD, 2001a).

The **employment rate for older workers**, in the age group 55–64 years, was 54.6 per cent in 2000. The average EU rate was 38.5 per cent.

## Part-time employment

In 2000, 15.7 per cent of Danish employees worked part time, i.e. less than 30 hours per week in their main job. This rate is lower than the average of 16.3 per cent for the EU-15, but higher than the OECD average of 15.3 per cent and the United States rate of 12.8 per cent. In the industrialized countries, part-time employment ranges from 5.4 per cent in Greece to 32.1 per cent in the Netherlands. In the same year, 23.5 per cent of employed women in Denmark worked part time, against 8.9 per cent of employed men (OECD, 2001a) (see figure 3 on page 13).

In contrast to most other countries, part-time employment in Denmark fell during the 1990s. In fact, it is the only country that has seen a marked reduction. The proportion of part-timers was 19.2 per cent in 1990. The part-time rate among women dropped by 6.1 per cent, accounting for a large part of the overall decline. The reasons are presumably linked to higher employment and reduced working time.

The level of part-time work (defined as less than full-time work) in Denmark is higher according to Eurostat sources (21.7 per cent in 2000), but the decline over the 1990s is confirmed by this source (Eurostat, 2001).

In 2000, 13.6 per cent of part-time employment in Denmark was rated as "involuntary", meaning that the jobholder would have preferred a full-time post. The rate is below the EU-15 average of 15.8 per cent, but there are countries with percentages as low as 3.5 per cent (Netherlands) and 9.7 per cent (United Kingdom) (Eurostat, 2001).

Eurostat provides data on the reasons why workers are in part-time employment. Of those who held part-time jobs in Denmark in 2000, 45.9 per cent were not seeking a full-time job because of family or other reasons (EU-15: 59.3 per cent), 34.7 per cent did not work full time because they were engaged in education or training (EU-15: 10.8 per cent), and 4.1 per cent preferred part-time employment for reasons of illness or disability (EU-15: 2.8 per cent) (Eurostat, 2001).

## Fixed-term employment

The proportion of workers in Denmark with employment contracts of limited duration was 10.2 per cent in 2000. This compares with a mean of 13.4 per cent in the EU-15. The rate for women was 11.7 per cent and for men 8.8 per cent (Eurostat, 2001).

## Unemployment

In 2000, approximately one worker in every 20 in the Danish labour force was unemployed. Using an internationally standardized measure, the **aggregate unemployment rate** stood at 4.7 per cent. In comparison, the average rate in the EU-15 was 8.3 per cent, and in the OECD-20, 6.6 per cent. Thus, Denmark is among the countries with comparatively low unemployment. Japan is at the same level as Denmark, while lower unemployment levels were recorded in the Netherlands (2.8 per cent), Norway (3.5 per cent), Austria (3.7 per cent), the United States (4.0 per cent), Portugal and Ireland (both 4.2 per cent) (OECD, 2001a) (see figure 4 on page 14).

The Danish unemployment rate was reduced by half during the 1990s. It has come down from 10.2 per cent in 1993 to less than 5 per cent in 2000. After Ireland and the Netherlands, Denmark was the next best performer in reducing unemployment in the 1990s.

The **unemployment rates for men and women** were 4.0 per cent and 5.0 per cent respectively in 2000. The **unemployment rate for young workers**, in the 15–24 year age group, was 6.7 per cent, compared with 15.6 per cent in the EU-15 (OECD, 2001a).

The **long-term unemployment rate** came down to 1.0 per cent in 1999, from 2.9 per cent in 1991. The EU-15 average rate was 3.6 per cent, with less than 1 per cent in Luxembourg (0.8 per cent) (ILO, 2002). The incidence of long-term unemployment (12 or more months) as a percentage of total unemployment was 20.0 per cent in Denmark in 2000, compared with an average of 46.6 in the EU-15 and 31.4 in the OECD (OECD, 2001a).

The **unemployment rate among foreigners** is higher than among nationals. In 2000, the unemployment rate of nationals was 4.3 per cent (8.2 per cent in the EU-15), but 13.5 per cent for non-nationals (Eurostat, 2001). However, the unemployment rate among foreigners has also declined since the mid-1990s. In 2000, the proportion of foreigners in the total labour force was 5.4 per cent (Statistics Denmark, 2000).

## Inactivity

The **inactivity rate** in the labour market is defined as the percentage of the population aged 25 to 54 years that is neither working nor seeking work (i.e. is not in the labour force). People in this age group are generally expected to be in the labour force, as they have normally completed their education and have not yet reached retirement age. If they are inactive, then they either cannot find jobs for economic reasons, or they prefer to stay out of the labour market. Thus, the inactivity rate in the "primary" age labour force provides important information supplementary to the employment and unemployment rates.

In 1999, Denmark's inactivity rate stood at 11.8 per cent, the second-lowest rate in the OECD after Iceland (see figure 5 on page 15). The other Nordic countries follow Denmark: Sweden 12.0 per cent; Finland 12.3 per cent; and Norway 12.4 per cent. The unweighted average inactivity rate for the EU-15 in 1999 was 17.6 per cent, and 17.1 per cent for the OECD-20 (ILO, 2002).

## Educational and vocational training

In 1999, 80 per cent of Denmark's labour force aged 25 to 64 years had completed at least **upper secondary education**, 20 per cent had completed type B **tertiary education** (in ISCED-97 levels) and 7 per cent type A tertiary education (see figure 6 on page 15). These educational attainments ranked the country in fifth, first, and penultimate position, respectively, among 20 OECD countries (OECD, 2001b).

Data for the **annual mean number of hours of job-related education and training per adult** are available for 11 OECD countries for the mid-1990s. With 91 hours, Denmark had the highest level ahead of New Zealand with 68 hours. The arithmetic average for the sample countries is 43 hours.

In a survey of the EU-15 undertaken in 1999, one question asked how many in the adult labour force (25–64 years) had participated in education and training in the previous four weeks. The proportion for Denmark was 20 per cent, second-highest after Sweden (26 per cent). The average for the EU was 8 per cent (Eurostat, 2001).

In 2000, 49 per cent of Danish employees undertook **training paid for or provided by their employer**. The highest proportion was recorded in Finland (55 per cent), while the EU-15 average was 33 per cent (European Foundation, 2001).

Participation of Danish youth in education is high. The proportion of 15–24-year-olds in education reached 70.9 per cent in 2000, the second-highest level in the EU after the Netherlands (71.7 per cent), and above the EU-15 average of 64.1 per cent. The rate for women in this age bracket was 72.3 per cent in Denmark, higher than in all other countries in Europe (EU-15 average: 65.4 per cent). Only 13.1 per cent of young Danes aged 25–34 years had stopped their education at lower secondary level (level I). This figure is among the lowest rates after Norway (7 per cent), the United Kingdom (10.5 per cent), and Sweden (12.8 per cent), and well below the mean EU-15 rate of 25.9 per cent (Eurostat, 2001).

**Total public expenditure on education as a percentage of GDP** in Denmark reached 6.8 per cent in 1998, the highest rate in the EU-15 with an average rate of 5.1 per cent (OECD, 2001b).

## Working hours

In 1999, the average collectively agreed weekly working time was 37 hours in Denmark and the Netherlands, among the lowest in Europe. The average weekly working time in the EU-15 was 38.6 hours (EIROnline).

In 2000, the Danes worked on average 36.1 hours per week (hours usually worked), compared with an average of 37.8 hours in the EU-15 (see figure 7 on page 16). Those who worked full time spent on average 40.6 hours at the workplace. This was over one hour less than the average in the European Union (41.7 hours). For those working part time, the average weekly hours were 13.7 for men and 21.8 for women, or an average of 19.8 hours (Eurostat, 2001).

The proportion of Danish employees engaged in **night work** is among the lowest in Europe. In 2000, 16 per cent of the Danish workforce reported that they worked at least one night per month. Only Italy and Portugal (both 15 per cent) had lower rates. The EU average stood at 19 per cent (European Foundation, 2001). In 2000, 6 per cent of Danish employees were usually on **shift work** (EU-15: 12.7 per cent), and 19.5 per cent of the employed usually performed **Sunday work** (EU-15: 11.4 per cent) (Eurostat, 2001).

The average number of **annual working hours** recorded in Denmark in 1998 was 1,527. This was the fourth-lowest recorded in the OECD countries after the Netherlands (1,368), Norway (1,444) and Austria (1,515). By comparison, the figure for the United States was 1,833. The unweighted average figure for the EU-15 was 1,641 hours and for the OECD-20 1,665 hours (Scarpetta et al., 2000).

Danish workers are entitled to 25 days (or 5 weeks) of **paid annual leave** (excluding national holidays) under the law, the same as in France, Sweden and Spain. The average amount of paid annual leave was 30 days in 2000. By comparison, statutory and average of collectively agreed entitlements were respectively 20 and 29.2 days in Germany, and 24 and 25 days in Sweden (EIROnline, working time developments, annual update, 2000).

## Level and growth of wages

In 2000, the hourly compensation cost for production workers in manufacturing in Denmark was US$20.44. This represented 88.9 per cent of the compensation cost in Germany (the highest in the world), but was still 10.5 per cent higher than the average for the European countries and 2.9 per cent above the level in the United States (Bureau of Labor Statistics, 2000a).

**Nominal hourly earnings** in the manufacturing sector grew at an average annual rate of 3.8 per cent between 1989 and 1999. In the 1980s, nominal growth averaged 7.2 per cent. **Real wages** grew by 1.6 per cent in the 1990s and 0.3 per cent in the 1980s (OECD, 2000a) (see figure 8 on page 17).

## Wage and income distribution

Unfortunately, internationally comparable data on wage and income distribution are available for only a limited number of countries and years. Nevertheless, the information available shows that Denmark is among the countries with the highest income equality.

The most common indicator for dispersion of income is the **Gini index**. Its value for Denmark was 24.7 in 1992, the latest year for which it was computed. Only one affluent country, Austria, was more egalitarian than Denmark. The index for Austria (measured in 1987) was 23.1. The value for Sweden was 25.0 (1992), the United Kingdom 36.1 (1991), and the United States 40.8 (1997) (UNDP, 2001).

In 1996, the Gini coefficient of inequality of net equivalent market income for Denmark was 0.43, the lowest value of a group of 13 EU countries (excluding Sweden and Finland). By comparison, Ireland and the United Kingdom had values around 0.52. Taking into account the effects of social benefits, Denmark arrived at a Gini coefficient of disposable income of 0.23, by far the lowest value of the group. The mean value for the EU-13 was 0.31. In no other country was the redistributive effect of social income as strong as in Denmark (Eurostat and European Commission, 2001).

The relatively high equality of income in Denmark is also mirrored in the proportions of income of the bottom and top quintiles of the population (see figure 9 on page 17). The proportion of total income of the bottom quintile was 11 per cent in 1996 (EU-15: 8 per cent). The values for the top quintile were 33 and 39 per cent respectively. The ratio of the proportion of total national income received by the top 20 per cent of the population to the bottom 20 per cent (80/20 ratio) is 2.9 in Denmark, the lowest value in the EU-15 where the average is 5.2 (Eurostat and European Commission, 2001).

A further indicator of distribution of household income is the **proportion of employed persons working full time, year round, and earning less than two-thirds of median earnings**. This measure is available for 12 OECD countries for one year only, 1993. Denmark's value on this indicator is 9.6 per cent, which is the second lowest level after Belgium (9.1 per cent). The largest values were found in the United Kingdom and the United States, with 21.0 and 26.3 per cent respectively (OECD, 1998a).

**Minimum wages** in Denmark are fixed by collective agreement. In 1997, the ratio of the minimum wage (exceeded by 95 per cent of wage earners) to

11

**Decent work in Denmark**

Figure 1    Labour force participation rate, 2000

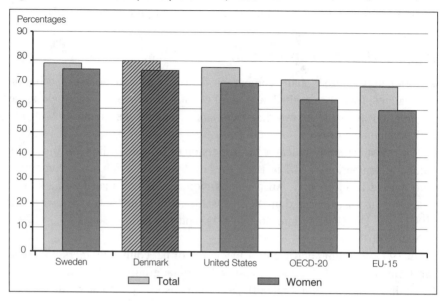

Source: OECD, 2001a.

Figure 2    Employment rate, 2000

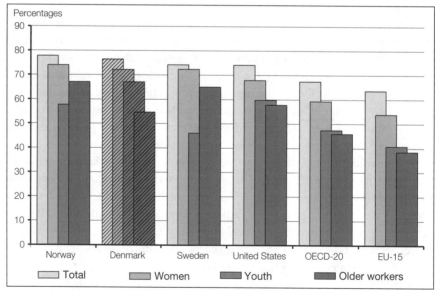

Source: OECD, 2001a.

Figure 3    Total part-time work as a percentage of total employment (A)
and part-time work of women (B), 1990 and 2000

A

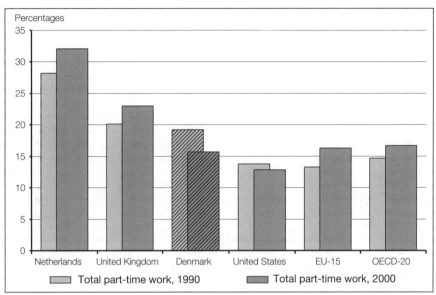

B

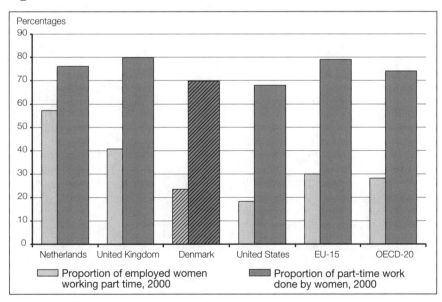

Source: OECD, 2001a.

**Decent work in Denmark**

Figure 4    Unemployment rates as a percentage of the labour force, 2000

A

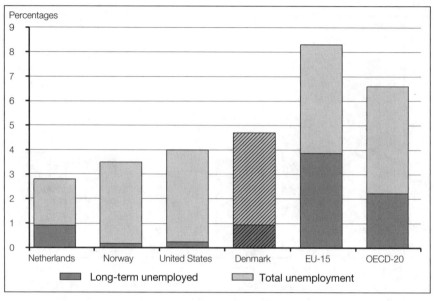

B

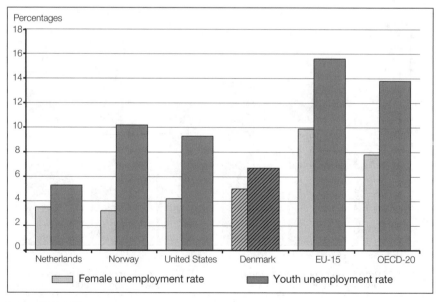

Source: OECD, 2001a.

Figure 5    Inactivity rate, 1999

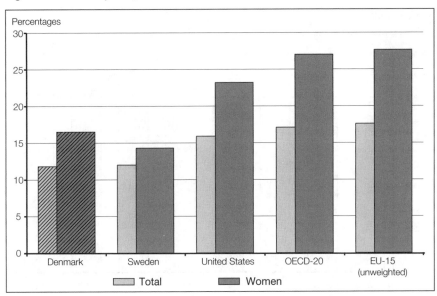

Source: ILO, 2002.

Figure 6    Level of educational attainment in the labour force, 1998

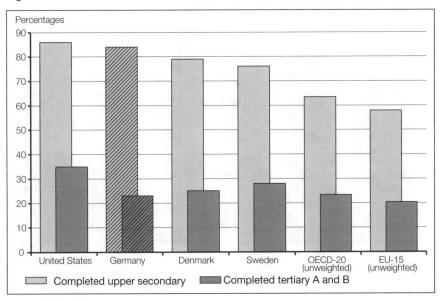

Source: OECD, 2001b.

## Figure 7 Annual and weekly average working hours, 1998 and 1999

### Annual hours

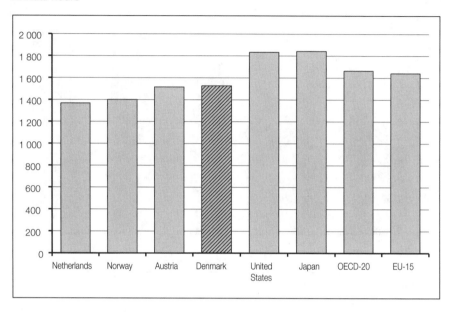

### Weekly hours

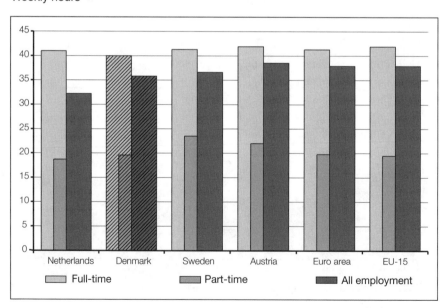

Source: Scarpetta et al., 2000; Eurostat, 2001.

Figure 8    Annual percentage change in real hourly earnings in manufacturing,
           1989–99

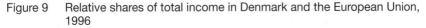
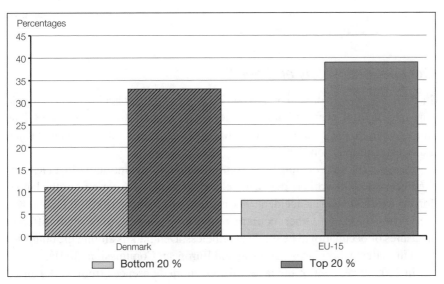

Source: OECD, 2000a.

Figure 9    Relative shares of total income in Denmark and the European Union,
           1996

Source: Eurostat and European Commission, 2001.

the average manufacturing wage was 53 per cent. This compares with 46 per cent in France, 45 per cent in the Netherlands, 31 per cent in the United States and 28 per cent in Japan (Danish Government, 2000, p. 337). Other sources show higher minimum to average wage ratios (for instance, for 1999 the Danish Confederation of Employers estimated a minimum wage of 68 per cent of the average wage in the manufacturing sector), but the relative differences between countries remain approximately the same (OECD, 1998a).

Denmark is among the countries with comparatively few people living in poverty. In the period 1993–95, 4.7 per cent of the Danish population had an equivalent household disposable income **of less than 50 per cent of the median equivalent household income** (defined as relative poverty), the lowest incidence among the EU and OECD countries included in the panel. The European average stood at 11.7 per cent, with 12.1 per cent in Germany and the United Kingdom, and 12.0 per cent in Spain. In Denmark, 9.1 per cent were poor at least once in this period, compared with 19.2 per cent in all European countries. Those who were always poor amounted to 0.8 per cent in Denmark and 3.8 per cent in other countries (OECD, 2001a).

In 1996, 11 per cent of the population in Denmark had an income less than 60 per cent of the national median equivalent. This was the lowest rate among the EU-15 countries, with an average of 17 per cent (Eurostat and European Commission, 2001).

In 1996, according to the Eurostat Community Household Panel, the **poverty rate among jobless households** in Denmark was 16 per cent. This was the lowest rate among the EU-15, with an average rate of 50 per cent (Eurostat and European Commission, 2001).

## Occupational safety and health

In 2000, 64 workers died in or as a consequence of a work accident in Denmark. The rate of **fatal occupational injuries** was 2.0 per 100,000 employees. The average rate for the period from 1993 to 2000 was 2.8 per 100,000 (Eurostat and European Commission, 2001).

In 2000, the rate of **non-fatal (temporary and permanent) injuries** was 1,623 per 100,000 workers per year, i.e. approximately 1.6 per cent of the labour force was affected by an accident. The average rate in the period 1993–2000 was 1,831 per 100,000. Other countries in Europe apply somewhat different measures of occupational health. Nevertheless, Denmark is among the countries with the safest workplaces (Eurostat and European Commission, 2001).

In 2000, 9 per cent of the labour force reported absences from work caused by work-related health problems. This figure was the same as the average for the EU-15. The range in the EU was from 18 per cent in Finland to 4 per cent in Portugal (European Foundation, 2001).

## Social protection and welfare

In 1998, 2.2 million Danes (of which 1.24 million were women), or slightly over 40 per cent of the total population, received some kind of public income transfer payment (Statistics Denmark, 2000). The average amount of benefits was 69,000 Danish crowns, or US$8,000. Taking only full-time equivalent public income transfer beneficiaries, the figure was 1.6 million people, or 30.2 per cent of the population. Some 28 per cent of all income transfer recipients are receiving temporary benefits, with the bulk of permanent benefits going in the form of old-age pensions. Transfers directly linked to unemployment or employment benefits concern 13 per cent of all beneficiaries (table 1).

Denmark provides very good **protection to unemployed persons**. Unemployment benefits are provided up to a level of 90 per cent of the previous wages for up to four years. However, there is a ceiling to the compensation, so that only the low-income groups reach the 90 per cent income replacement level. In 1997, the net compensation rates for an average industrial worker were 63 per cent for a single person, 67 per cent for a married couple, 75 per cent for a single parent with two children, and 77 per cent for a couple with two children. In addition, unemployment benefits are not fully taxed. In Sweden, the range was from 72 to 90 per cent, in Finland from 60 to 84 per cent. The average income replacement rate for unemployment benefits in Denmark was estimated at 70 per cent, while the average for the EU-15 was 60 per cent and for OECD countries 58 per cent. Sweden had a rate of 75 per cent, Spain and Switzerland 73 per cent. Denmark had the longest duration of benefit payment. In terms of the percentage of unemployed workers receiving benefits, Denmark ranked third after Sweden and Spain (OECD, 1999). About 85 per cent of the unemployed in Denmark are covered by unemployment insurance (Madsen, 2001).

In contrast to the highly developed income protection for the unemployed, the statutory provisions for **employment protection** in Denmark are comparatively moderate. When an employment contract is terminated, the average period of notice is 1.8 months after 9 months of employment with the same employer; 3 months notice after 4 years of employment; and 4.3 months notice after 20 years of employment. On average, severance pay is provided only after 20 years of employment at an average rate of 1.5 months' salary. However, notice periods and severance pay vary according to collective agreements and individual contracts. By comparison, after 20 years of employment, the

Table 1    Percentage distribution of full-time equivalent income transfer
           recipients by type of benefit in Denmark, 1998

| Benefits | Percentage |
|---|---|
| **Temporary** | **27.62** |
| Unemployment | 9.01 |
| Sickness | 3.12 |
| Maternity | 2.16 |
| Cash benefit | 5.68 |
| Rehabilitation | 1.35 |
| Local employment scheme | 2.58 |
| Public employment service | 1.44 |
| Leave | 2.28 |
| **Permanent** | **72.38** |
| Old-age pension | 43.98 |
| Early retirement pension | 16.92 |
| Early retirement pay | 11.48 |
| **Total** | **100.00** |

Source: Statistics Denmark, 2000.

mandatory severance pay amounts to 12 months' salary in Spain, 18 months in Italy and 20 months in Portugal (OECD, 1999).

The **pension system** in Denmark consists of four pillars:

(1) a tax-financed public old-age pension independent of years of employment and previous income; in 1998, it covered 99 per cent of those of pension age;
(2) a supplementary pension based on years of employment (the labour market supplementary pension fund), mandated by law and financed by the contributions of employers (two-thirds) and employees (one-third);
(3) an income-based labour market pension regulated through collective agreements; these cover 63 per cent of pensioners; the pension funds are administered by the social partners, particularly the trade unions;
(4) private pension schemes, covering 34 per cent of those of pension age.

Old-age pension is payable to people aged 67 years and over; this will change to 65 years and over as of 2004. Most pensioners are entitled to the first three benefits, with a growing percentage also benefiting from a private pension scheme.

The public old-age pension consists of a basic rate and a pension supplement. On 1 January 2001, the basic monthly rate was 4,260 Danish crowns (i.e. US$500), and the pension supplement 4,290 crowns.

Semi-retirement pensions may be paid to wage earners and self-employed people between the ages of 60 and 65 years, who reduce their working hours, but remain in active employment, with permanent residence in Denmark.

Recipients of public old-age pensions and early retirement pensions may be granted individual supplements for health care and heating, as well as housing subsidies and child benefits.

**Sickness benefits** in Denmark are paid for 52 weeks in any one-and-a-half-year period (but can be extended under special circumstances). There is no qualifying day for receiving the compensation. This compares with an unlimited duration of benefit payment in Sweden, 78 weeks in any three years in Germany, 52 weeks in the Netherlands, and 28 weeks in the United Kingdom. There is one qualifying day in Sweden, none in Germany, two days in the Netherlands, and three days in the United Kingdom. In Denmark, full or nearly full wage payment during illness is provided for by collective agreements. It is estimated that between 60 and 65 per cent of employees enjoy full pay when on sick leave.

In an OECD survey of citizens' satisfaction with national health services, 90 per cent of respondents in Denmark said that they were "highly or very satisfied". This was the highest percentage among the EU countries (OECD, 1998d).

Women are entitled to 14 weeks of **maternity leave** from work, of which two weeks are compulsory. Fathers are entitled to up to four weeks' paternity leave. One of the parents is entitled to up to 10 weeks of parental leave. Public sector employees receive full wage compensation during maternity or parental leave as part of their collective agreements. Some collective agreements in the private sector also grant compensation.

**Childcare leave** for persons with children aged up to 8 years is granted either as a statutory or collective agreement benefit to wage earners, and those who are self-employed or unemployed. The self-employed can benefit only from the statutory provisions. For children up to 1 year of age, each parent has an individual right to a minimum of eight weeks, and a maximum of 26 weeks' leave. For children over 1 year, the maximum is 13 weeks. Wage earners have the option to negotiate additional leave with their employer, although the total leave period can never exceed 52 weeks. During childcare leave the parent is entitled to a benefit amounting to 60 per cent of the highest unemployment benefit.

In the event of total **disability**, and hence complete loss of working capacity, Denmark and Sweden have a very high replacement rate for single people on average incomes.

Denmark has a comprehensive **social assistance (cash welfare benefits)** scheme, which provides an economic safety net for people who are unable to support themselves. The amount of social assistance depends on the household income and the individual's capital. The maximum rate is 10,243 crowns per month. In all the Nordic countries, the index of average net social assistance benefits after housing costs exceeds 120 per cent of per capita GDP, while the proportion of recipients in the national population is between 3 and 10 per cent. In particular, social assistance includes subsidies to families with children, provision of publicly funded childcare services, and services for the elderly. However, social assistance benefits are conditional, when applicable, on participation in labour market training and rehabilitation programmes.

In 2000, **recipients of social transfers (as main income)** amounted to 22.5 per cent of the working-age population (Madsen, 2001). They had reached a maximum of 26 per cent in 1995. The largest share of the transfers were in the form of disability benefits, followed by compensation under the early retirement scheme and the unemployment benefit scheme. The numbers of people on long-term sick leave or on early retirement have been increasing in Denmark and other Nordic countries. This can be linked to changes in working life, especially stress at work, as well as to financial incentives linked to early retirement. The fact that fewer people are staying in work until the statutory retirement age, at a time when the population is ageing rapidly, has become a serious concern in Nordic and other European countries (Gabriel and Liimatainen, 2000).

Taking all publicly mandated welfare provisions together, **total public social security expenditure** reached 33.0 per cent of GDP in 1996 (figure 10). This includes expenditure on pensions, health care, employment injury, sickness, family assistance, housing and social assistance in cash and kind. Denmark had the second highest level of social spending in the OECD, behind Sweden (34.7 per cent) and ahead of Finland (32.3 per cent) and France (30.1 per cent). Between 1985 and 1996, social expenditure in Denmark increased by 7.1 percentage points. At the bottom of the distribution among the affluent countries are the United States, Australia and Japan, which in the mid-1990s spent respectively 16.5, 15.7 and 14.1 per cent of their GDP on social welfare. The Danish expenditure level is far above the unweighted average of 24.0 per cent for the OECD-20 countries, and 26.2 per cent for the EU-15. The percentage of Danish GDP spent on pensions was 9.6 per cent, and on health care 5.2 per cent. Total social security expenditure represented 52.5 per cent of total public expenditure (ILO, 2000).

**Employee social security contributions,** as a percentage of wages, were 10 per cent in Denmark, close to the averages of the OECD-20 (8.9 per cent) and of 14 EU countries (10.7 per cent).

**Employer social security contributions** in Denmark, as in Australia and New Zealand, were nil in 1997. This compares with an average of 14.8 per cent in the OECD-20 and 18.9 per cent in 14 EU countries (OECD, 1998b).

Figure 10   Total public social security expenditure as a percentage of GDP, mid-1990s

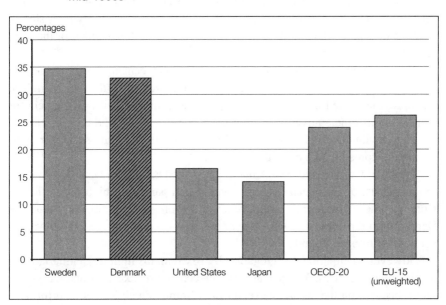

Source: ILO, 2000.

## Gender equality

Gender equality here refers to the relative opportunities of women and men in the labour market along the following dimensions: (1) access to education, training and employment; (2) access to particular job positions in specific occupations and sectors; and (3) ranking in terms of occupational status, promotion opportunities, earnings and social security coverage. Indicators of "horizontal" and "vertical" labour market segregation measure the gap between women and men on the latter two dimensions.

Women's **educational level** in Denmark is nearly as high as that of men. The proportion of the population aged 25–64 years that had completed at least upper secondary education in 1999 was 76 per cent for women and 83 per cent for men. The OECD averages were respectively 58 and 63 per cent. However, for the age group 25–34 years, the proportion of women, at 87 per cent, was only one percentage point lower than for men. Some 27 per cent of women and 26 per cent of men in the 25–64-year age group completed at least tertiary education, against 21 and 23 per cent on average in the OECD (OECD, 2001b).

**Labour force participation** of women and men has steadily moved towards convergence over the past 40 years. In 1960, virtually all men of working age were in the labour force, whereas the rate for women was just 43.5 per cent. By 2000, the rate for men was 84 per cent, and for women 75.9 per cent (figure 11). Between 1981 and 1999, the difference in activity rates shrank from 14 to 8 percentage points. In 1998, the proportion of women in the total labour force (aged 15 years and above) reached 46.3 per cent.

The **employment rate** of women was 72.1 per cent in 2000, among the highest in Europe, but still 8.6 percentage points less than that for men. The unemployment rate for women was 5.0 per cent, compared with 4.0 per cent for men. The full-time equivalent employment rate of women in the EU is closely correlated with the employment rate of women in personal and social services. Denmark scores highest on both variables.

Together with Finland, Sweden and the United Kingdom, Denmark is at the top of the list of European countries with a comparatively high proportion of workers whose **immediate supervisor** is a woman. In 2000, the value for Denmark on this indicator was 28 per cent. The average for the EU-15 was 19 per cent (European Foundation, 2001).

However, occupational segregation by sex remains high in Denmark, as in many other countries. Women are 75 per cent more likely to enter a public sector occupation than a private sector one. In municipalities, women form 77 per cent of all employees (table 2).

Over 80 per cent of women employees are concentrated in four of 10 occupational groups (figure 12). Danish women are well represented among technicians, clerks, service workers, and plant and machine operators and assemblers. Women in Denmark are less well positioned in **higher**

Figure 11   Labour force participation rate in Denmark by sex, 1960–2000

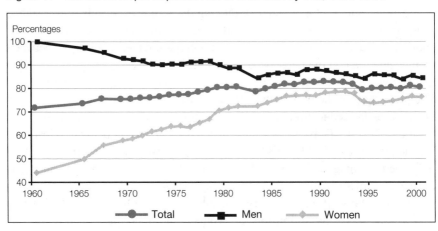

Source: OECD, 2000b; ILO, 2002.

Table 2      Percentage of women in different employment sectors in Denmark, 1999

| Sector | Percentage of women |
| --- | --- |
| Total labour force (16–66 years) | 46.1 |
| Wage earners | 47.6 |
| Private sector | 37.1 |
| Public sector | 65.1 |
| Central government | 42.6 |
| Municipalities | 76.9 |

Source: Statistics Denmark, 2000.

Figure 12   Proportion of women in different occupational groups (ISCO-88) in Denmark, 1998

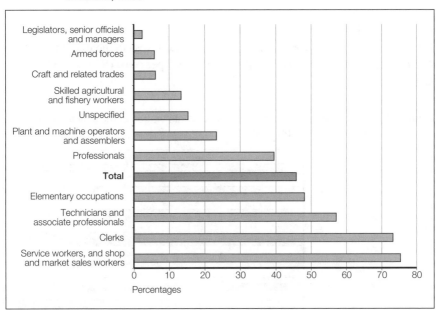

Source: ILO, 2001a.

**administrative and managerial jobs**. Women hold fewer than 3 per cent of positions as legislators, senior officials and managers.

Yet, in parliament, women hold 37.4 per cent of all seats. They held 45 per cent of all ministerial posts in 1999. This ranks Denmark just behind Sweden (55.0 per cent). In the national government appointed in December 2000, 9 out of 21 cabinet ministers (42.8 per cent) were women (UNDP, 2001).

Denmark's record of **women entrepreneurs** is comparatively poor. Only 21.4 per cent of entrepreneurs were women in the period 1990–99, the fourth-lowest among 27 OECD countries. Portugal had 41 per cent, and 11 other countries had rates between 30 per cent and 40 per cent (OECD, 2000b).

A useful indicator of the relative earnings position of women is the **gender wage gap**, measured as the difference between average earnings of women and those of men (figure 13). In 1998, women in industry and services in Denmark earned on average 82 per cent of average male earnings. A similar gender wage gap was observed in Belgium, France, Finland and Sweden. In Austria, the Netherlands and the United Kingdom, the ratio of women's earnings to men's was around 70 per cent. The average for the EU-15 was 77 per cent (Eurostat and European Commission, 2001).

Another source on earnings differentials by sex yields an aggregate ratio of 0.70 for female to male earnings. This is the highest ratio observed worldwide (UNDP, 2001).

The gap between female and male wages in Denmark is highest in the private sector (on average 17 per cent in 1999). It is less in the municipal sector (13 per cent), and still less in the state sector (8.5 per cent) (Statistics Denmark, 2001).

Figure 13   Female wages as a percentage of male wages in the private and state sectors, Denmark, 1996

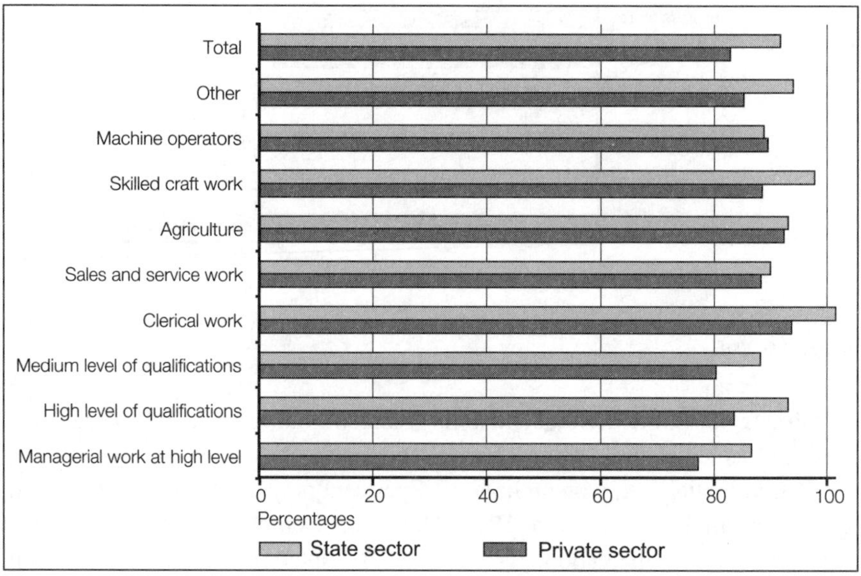

Source: Statistics Denmark, 1998.

A study of **overall performance on gender equality** in the labour market, based on the distribution of paid and unpaid work and the position of women in the labour market in EU countries in 1997, gave Denmark and Sweden the highest scores. Both countries reached an index of 0.54, compared with 0.31 for the EU-15 (Plantenga and Hansen, 1999).

## Fundamental rights at work and international labour standards

Denmark has ratified all the fundamental international labour Conventions, covering freedom of association and collective bargaining (No. 87 and No. 98), the elimination of forced and compulsory labour (No. 29 and No. 105), the elimination of discrimination in respect of remuneration, employment and occupation (No. 100 and No. 111), and the abolition of child labour (No. 138 and No. 182). It has also ratified other major Conventions on labour market policies such as the Employment Policy Convention (No. 122), the Labour Inspection Conventions (No. 81 and No. 129), the Tripartite Consultation Convention (No. 144), the Labour Administration Convention (No. 150), the Vocational Rehabilitation and Employment (Disabled Persons) Convention (No. 159), the Labour Statistics Convention (No. 160), the Occupational Safety and Health Conventions (No. 152, No. 155, No. 167) and the Indigenous and Tribal Peoples Convention (No. 169).

As of 31 July 2001, Denmark had ratified 67 ILO Conventions, of which 59 were in force. This is a relatively low number compared with Finland (79 Conventions in force out of 95 ratified), Sweden (73 in force, 89 ratified), Norway (90 in force, 105 ratified), and France (96 in force, 115 ratified). Denmark's relatively low ratification record can be ascribed to a preference for regulating the labour market via collective bargaining agreements rather than by law.

During the past 20 years, about 25 complaints of violation of ILO Conventions were filed against the Danish Government. In part, they concerned the application of the Freedom of Association and Protection of the Right to Organise Convention (No. 87 of 1948) and the Right to Organise and Collective Bargaining Convention (No. 98 of 1949), in as much as the Government intervened repeatedly in both private and public sector collective bargaining processes to resolve disputes between the bargaining parties. This occurred most recently in spring of 1998, when the Government enacted a law to end a conflict over additional leave that threatened to escalate into a general strike. The ILO Governing Body Committee on Freedom of Association considered that the statutory renewal and extension of collective agreements, provided for by the labour law when the parties fail to reach agreement and to which the Government is repeatedly resorting, was not in conformity with the principles of free collective bargaining and the right of workers' and employers' organizations to organize their activities and to formulate their programmes, and might also have a negative impact on the right to strike. In all the cases, the Committee on Freedom of Association called on the Government to refrain from taking such measures in future.

Through the bodies charged with the regular supervision of the observance by member States of their standard-related obligations, the ILO maintains a positive and constructive dialogue with the Government and the social partners on the application of all ratified Conventions by Denmark. (For more detailed information see the ILO database on international labour standards (ILOLEX), accessible through the ILO Website, http://www.ilo.org).

## Collective organization, collective bargaining and collective action

The great majority of wage and salary earners in Denmark are members of a trade union. In 1994, the **net trade union density rate**, measuring the number of trade union members as a percentage of all wage earners, was 80.1 per cent. Sweden (91.1 per cent) and Finland (79.3 per cent) are the other two countries in the OECD where more than two-thirds of the labour force are organized (figure 14). A second group includes countries where the trade union density is around 50 per cent: Norway (57.7 per cent), Belgium (51.9 per cent) and Ireland (48.9 per cent). At the bottom end of the scale are countries such as the United States (14.2 per cent) and France (9.1 per cent). The EU-15 unweighted average stood at 43.0 per cent, while the average rate for the OECD-20 was 39.7 per cent (ILO, 1997; OECD, 1997). It should be noted, however, that the trade union density rate is not necessarily a good indicator of trade union strength, influence, and capacity for collective action. One reason for the high membership rates in the Nordic countries (and also in Belgium) relates to the unemployment benefit administration managed by the trade unions.

In the period between the mid-1980s and the mid-1990s, the trade union density rate in Denmark increased by 1.8 percentage points. The Swedish unions gained 7.3 points, the Finnish unions 11 points, the Norwegian unions 2.0 points, the Spanish unions 7.1 points, and the Canadian unions 0.7 points. In all other OECD countries, unions faced a net loss of membership. The trade unions in the Nordic countries have been more successful than elsewhere in organizing women, white-collar workers and part-time workers (Ebbinghaus and Visser, 2000).

In a survey conducted in 1999, 50 per cent of the Danish population expressed trust in trade unions, whereas 38 per cent tended not to trust them and 12 per cent did not voice an opinion. A higher level of trust was encountered in

Figure 14   Social dialogue in the mid-1990s (percentages of wage and salary earners)

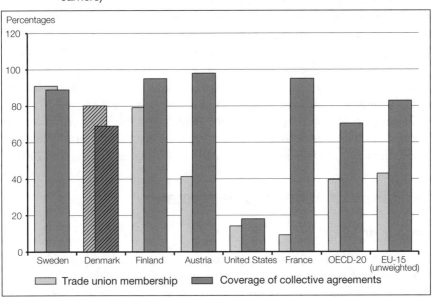

Sources: OECD, 1997; ILO, 2000.

the Netherlands (60 per cent) and Finland (54 per cent), while in the EU-15 the rate was only 35 per cent, and 49 per cent for non-trust (Eurostat and European Commission, 2001).

There is less complete information about **employer organization density rates**. In 1995, the member firms of the Danish Employers' Confederation (DA) covered about half of the labour force in the private sector, and some 70 per cent in the manufacturing sector, but much lower proportions in services. The employer density rate in the economy as a whole is estimated at 72 per cent (Visser, 1998, quoted in Visser, 2001).

The **proportion of workers directly covered by collective agreements** in Denmark in the period 1990 to 1994 was recorded at 69 per cent. A more recent survey commissioned by the Danish Confederation of Trade Unions (LO) showed that the collective agreement coverage rate reached 83 per cent in 2000 (LO, 2000a). Comparable rates were given for Austria (98 per cent) and the Netherlands (81 per cent in 1994), and lower rates for the United Kingdom (47 per cent), Japan (21 per cent) and the United States (18 per cent).

The **strike rate** in Denmark was below the EU average in every year between 1990 and 1997. In 1998, there were 1,317 days lost per 1,000 employees as the result of an 11-day strike that brought the average annual rate for the period

1990–98 up to 184 days per 1,000 employees. The EU average in the same period was 99 days per 1,000 employees.

According to the European Survey on Working Conditions, Danish workers exert relatively great **influence over working conditions**. For example, 58 per cent of people interviewed felt that they could influence their working hours. This was the highest proportion in the EU-15, where the average was 45 per cent. Eighty-four per cent of Danish workers said that they had the possibility of discussing organizational changes. Again this rate was above the EU-15 rate of 71 per cent. Finally, 77 per cent of the Danish workforce, compared with 75 per cent of all European Union workers, reported that, when consultation took place, it led to improvements in the workplace (European Foundation, 2001).

# Indicators of economic performance

## Labour productivity

In 2000, the **GDP per person employed** in Denmark was US$50,116 in 1995 terms (at purchasing power parity (PPP)), which placed the country just below the average for the OECD-20. Six other European countries had values close to the Danish one, including Germany, Sweden and Norway. Higher productivity levels were achieved in the United States (US$67,604), Belgium (US$63,821) and Ireland (US$60,881) (OECD, 2001c).

Denmark performs better if productivity is measured as **GDP per hour worked**. In 1998, this indicator reached US$32.3 (at PPP), placing the country in ninth position in the OECD-20. The United States attained US$36.3. The highest hourly productivity values were recorded for Norway (US$39.5) and Belgium (US$39.5). The reason behind the higher ranking of Denmark on the hourly productivity measure lies in its comparatively low number of annual working hours (Scarpetta et al., 2000).

Any assessment of performance measured in terms of labour productivity has to take into account some structural features. One of them is the composition of economic sectors, another the average size of enterprises. Being a small economy and a small-firm economy, Denmark will – other things being equal – have lower productivity levels than a country with a higher proportion of large enterprises with their corresponding superior economies of scale.

## Prosperity

In 2000, the *gross domestic product per capita (in PPP)* of Denmark was US$28,300. This placed Denmark among the most prosperous countries in the

EU-15 (behind Luxembourg and Ireland), and at sixth most prosperous among the industrialized countries (behind Luxembourg, Ireland, the United States, Norway and Switzerland).

Denmark was already among the most affluent countries in the 1960s. In 1970, it had the seventh highest GDP per capita among the OECD countries, but by 1980 lost ground, falling to twelfth position. By 1990, it had moved up to rank 11, and subsequently recovered strongly to regain a level of prosperity near the top of the European and OECD scales.

## Economic growth

Over the period 1993–2000, real GDP grew at an average rate of 3.1 per cent per year. This compares with 1.9 per cent per year from 1983 to 1993. The average annual rate of growth of real GDP per capita in Denmark in the period 1989–99 was 1.7 per cent, which was below the 2.0 per cent of the United States, slightly lower than the 1.8 per cent unweighted average for the OECD-20, and marginally higher than the EU-15 average of 1.6 per cent. In the 1980s, GDP per capita increased at an annual rate of 1.4 per cent, and in the 1970s at 1.2 per cent, both lower than the EU-15 and OECD-20 averages (IMF, 2001; OECD, 2000a).

## Inflation

Consumer prices in Denmark rose by 2.5 per cent in 1999 and 3.0 per cent in 2000. The average rate of inflation over the 1990s was 2.1 per cent, while in the 1980s it was 6.9 per cent. A peak rate of 12.0 per cent was reached in 1981 (Statistics Denmark).

## Taxation

Total tax revenue in Denmark reached 49.8 per cent of GDP in 1998, the second-highest rate after Sweden (52.0 per cent). The average EU-15 rate was 41.3 per cent, while the rate in the United States was 28.9 per cent. Tax revenue has increased only marginally in Denmark, by 2 percentage points since 1989–91. The distinguishing feature of taxation in Denmark is that it bears essentially on incomes and on goods and services, with little or no tax on wages and payrolls (figure 15). Taxes on incomes and profits represented 58.9 per cent of total revenue in 1998 (34.8 per cent in the EU-15 and 49.5 per cent in the United States), whereas taxes on goods and services amounted to 33.2 per cent (30.2 per cent in the EU-15 and 16.2 per cent in the United States). Conversely, social security taxes represented only 3.1 per cent of total revenue in Denmark,

Figure 15   Tax revenue by main headings as a percentage of total taxation, 1998

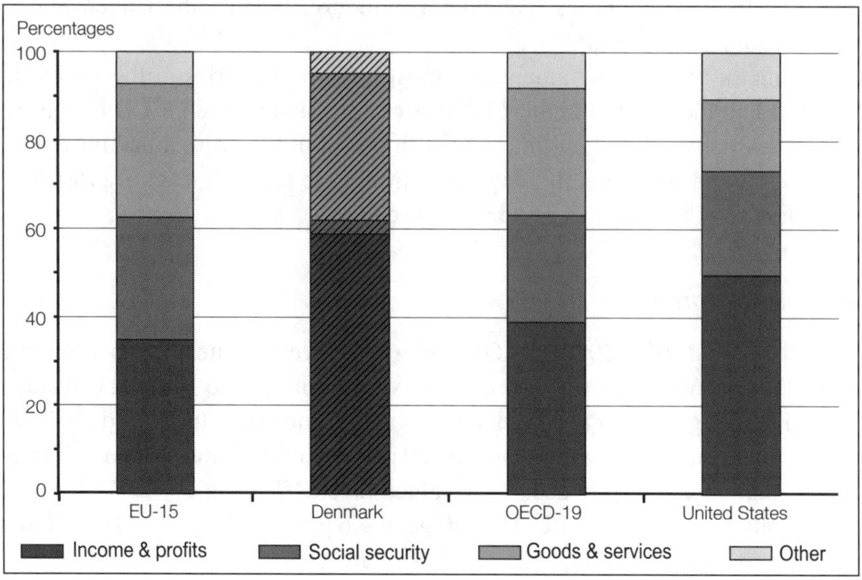

Percentages

Source: OECD, 2000c.

against 27.8 per cent in the EU-15 and 23.7 per cent in the United States (OECD, 2000c).

**Corporate income taxes** are comparatively low in Denmark, representing 5.6 per cent of total taxation in 1998, compared with 9.0 per cent in the United States and 8.7 per cent in the EU-15.

The income tax and employee social security contributions amounted to 45 per cent of the gross wage of a single worker (at average production worker income level) in Denmark in 1997, and 32 per cent for a single-earner couple (including transfers). This was by far the highest among the OECD countries. Combining income tax and employee/employer social security contributions as a percentage of the gross wage of a single earner, the proportion in Denmark remains unchanged at 45 per cent, but the country moves to eighth position (OECD, 1998b).

The **average rate of income tax** in Denmark was 38.7 per cent in 1995, far higher than in any other industrialized country. By comparison, the rate was 32.2 per cent in Finland, 31.9 per cent in Sweden, 27.3 per cent in Germany, 36.3 per cent in the United States, 27.0 per cent for the OECD countries as a whole, and 27.4 per cent for all EU countries. Income taxation in Denmark is highly progressive: the highest marginal income tax rate is 63.2 per cent, again the highest in the OECD countries (EU average: 46.5 per cent).

The average effective consumption tax rate is 19.6 per cent, compared with 17.9 per cent in the EU and 7.6 per cent in the United States. At 25 per cent, value-added tax rates in Denmark and Sweden are the highest in the EU-15. The range is between 15 and 25 per cent.

## Fiscal and trade balance

The fiscal balance of the central government in Denmark moved from a deficit in the first half of the 1990s to a surplus as of 1997, reaching 2.8 per cent of GDP in 2000 (table 3). The combined fiscal position of the EU countries turned positive only in 2000 (0.6 per cent of GDP) following a large deficit in 1993, which subsequently declined steadily. The United States registered a surplus as of 1999.

The gross and net government financial liabilities as a percentage of GDP in 2000 amounted to 49.8 and 26.4 per cent, respectively. By comparison, the gross and net rates of public debt for the EU-15 were 70.2 and 50.3 per cent, and for the United States, 58.8 and 43.0 per cent (OECD, 2001c).

In 2000, Denmark recorded a surplus of US$2.3 billion (or 2.6 per cent of GDP) on its current account balance of payments. During the 1990s, surpluses were recorded on the current account in every year except 1998, whereas deficits had prevailed throughout the period 1975–85, with a peak in the level of deficit in 1986. The Danish economy has run a positive trade balance since 1987. The foreign debt (as a percentage of GDP) was at a maximum in the mid-1980s.

Taking these indicators together, it appears that the country's public finances are in comparatively good health.

## Business environment and competitiveness

The Economist Intelligence Unit (EIU), which ranks countries in terms of their business environment, placed Denmark in position 11 of 60 countries, and 6 in Europe, for the period 1996–2000. It is forecast that, in the period 2001–5, Denmark will improve its standing to eighth position on the global scale, remaining at sixth on the regional scale. The EIU identified the following features of the Danish business environment; a predictable and stable macro-economic and political environment; a positive policy stance towards private enterprise, competition and foreign investment; an excellent infrastructure; and a well-functioning banking and finance sector. A recent tax reform, enabling international companies to repatriate their dividends from Danish subsidiaries free of tax, will attract more foreign companies and investment in the coming years. The finance sector is expected to grow strongly owing to accelerating

Table 3    Comparison of core economic and social indicators in Denmark, the United States, the EU and the OECD[a]

| Indicator | Year | Country or average | | | | Source |
|---|---|---|---|---|---|---|
| | | Denmark | EU | OECD-20 | United States | |
| Labour force participation (% pop. 15–64) | 2000 | 80.0 | 69.5 | 72.2 | 77.2 | OECD (2001a) |
| Employment rate (% pop. 15–64) | 2000 | | | | | |
|   *Total* | | 76.4 | 63.6 | 67.4 | 74.1 | OECD (2001a) |
|   *Women* | | 72.1 | 53.9 | 59.3 | 67.9 | OECD (2001a) |
|   *Youth* | | 67.1 | 40.8 | 47.4 | 59.8 | OECD (2001a) |
| Unemployment rate (% labour force) | 2000 | | | | | |
|   *Total* | | 4.5 | 8.4 | 6.7 | 4.0 | OECD (2001a) |
|   *Women* | | 5.0 | 9.9 | 7.8 | 4.2 | OECD (2001a) |
|   *Long-term* | 1999 | 1.0 | 3.6 | 2.8 | 0.3 | ILO (2002) |
| Inactivity rate (% pop. 25–54) | 1999 | 11.8 | 17.6[b] | 17.1 | 15.9 | ILO (2002) |
| Income inequality (Gini index) | 1992 | 24.7 | ... | ... | 40.8 (1997) | ILO (2002) |
| Social security expenditure (% GDP) | 1996 | 33.0 | 26.2[b] | 24.0 | 16.5 | ILO (2000) |
| Gender equality index | 1997 | 0.54 | 0.31 | ... | ... | Plantenga and Hansen (1999) |
| Trade union density rate (% wage and salary earners) | 1994–95 | 80.1 | 43.0[b] | 39.7 | 14.2 | ILO (1997) |
| Annual hours worked | 1998 | 1 527 | 1 641[b] | 1 665 | 1 833 | Scarpetta et al. (2000) |
| GDP per employed person (1995 US$ at PPP) | 1998 | 49 398 | 52 268 | 50 821 | 66 638 | Scarpetta et al. (2000) |
| GDP per hour worked (1995 US$ at PPP) | 1998 | 32.3 | 32.3 | 30.8 | 36.3 | Scarpetta et al. (2000) |
| GDP per capita (1995 US$ at PPP) | 1998 | 25 237 | 21 333 | 22 260[b] | 32 554 | Scarpetta et al. (2000) |
| Inflation (annual average change) | 1989–99 | 2.1 | 3.3 | 3.2 | 3.0 | OECD (2001a) |
| Fiscal balance (% of GDP) | 2000 | 2.8 | 0.6 | 2.6 | 1.7 | OECD (2001a) |
| Average annual growth in real GDP (%) | 1989–99 | 2.1 | 1.9 | 2.5 | 3.0 | OECD (2001a) |

[a] Where not otherwise indicated, EU values are harmonized averages of the EU members. OECD-20 figures are unweighted averages of 20 OECD developed countries: EU (barring Luxembourg), Australia, Canada, Japan, New Zealand, Norway, United States.

[b] Unweighted average.

... not available or not meaningful.

Nordic mergers and acquisitions. Further labour market and taxation reforms are being phased in gradually (Economist Intelligence Unit, 2001).

According to international surveys, Danish citizens, as well as the business community, are satisfied with public sector institutions, including the tax-financed services. Company managers give the bureaucracy the highest scores of all industrialized countries surveyed, and show a very high regard for the national political system's adaptation to economic changes (Danish Government, 2000).

It is relatively easy to start a business in Denmark. According to an index measuring the regulatory steps and time required for approval to start a business, the country has by far the best rating among the EU-15. In 1999, it attained a value of 0.2 on this index, while Sweden had a value of close to 0.8, Finland had slightly more than 0.8, Germany 1.2, and Spain close to 1.4. Danish business start-up procedures involve only two steps (Larsson, 1999).

The Global Competitiveness Report 2000 (World Economic Forum, 2001) ranked Denmark in sixth position among 58 countries, up from seventh place in 1999. Ahead of Denmark were Finland, the United States, Germany, the Netherlands and Switzerland.

The use of information and communication technology in industry is very advanced in Denmark. For example, in 1999, in firms with 20 employees and more, 90 per cent used the Internet (ILO, 2001b). In the population as a whole, the rate of Internet penetration was just over 50 per cent in 2000, more than double the rate in 1998. Only in Sweden is there a higher proportion of Internet users (60 per cent). Moreover, in 2000, Denmark was one of six countries in the EU-15 in which the percentage of people living in households with a mobile phone was over 60 per cent, compared with an average of 55 per cent in the EU (Eurostat and European Commission, 2001).

## Progress and setbacks

Historically, there has been a sustained rise in living standards in Denmark, as can be seen from figure 16 and table 4. Over the period 1913–92, GDP per capita increased at an annual rate of 2.0 per cent, a fivefold increase overall, in line with the Western European performance, but superior to that of the United States. The "Golden Age", from 1950 to 1973, stands out in particular for the high growth in GDP per capita and in labour productivity. However, during the period 1974–83, Denmark registered unemployment levels and consumer price inflation higher than the European averages or the United States levels. Likewise, the increase in life expectancy of 3.6 years between 1960 and 1998 was almost 50 per cent lower than the average increase in Germany, Sweden and the United States.

Figure 16   GDP per capita in Denmark, 1960–98 (1998 US$ at PPP)

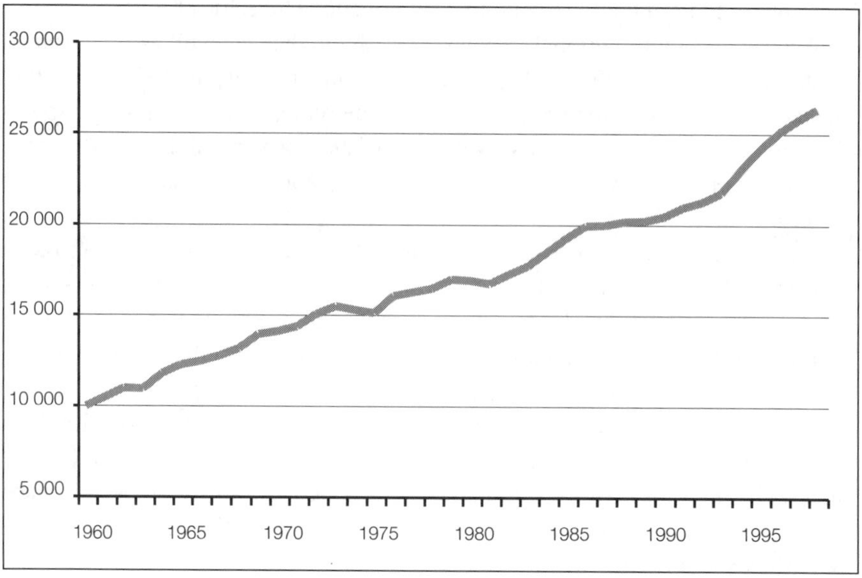

Source: Bureau of Labor Statistics, 2000b.

During 1973–93, the country went through some critical periods, during which both the economic and social performance and the social consensus were much weaker. In the 1970s and 1980s, Denmark – along with other countries of the European Economic Community (EEC) – suffered from low economic growth and rising unemployment (figure 17). Nominal wage growth soared in the 1970s, and was still at a high level in the 1980s, without any commensurate real increase in wages. In fact, in the 1990s, despite much lower nominal wage increases, the rate of real wage improvement was higher than in the 1980s. Inflation had reached 12 per cent per year in 1981, and unemployment peaked in 1993. Between 1987 and 1993, Denmark went through a deep recession, caused partly by internal policies (including an overvalued currency, excessive credit expansion, large fiscal deficit and high inflation rates), and partly by the failure of the fixed-band exchange rate under the European Monetary System, and high interest rates. In that period, real GDP increased by an average of 0.6 per cent per year, the level of employment shrank by 3.5 per cent, and unemployment rose by 4.5 percentage points to 12.4 per cent in 1993 (IMF, 2000). The recession in Denmark was deeper than in the EU as a whole, but less severe than in Finland and Sweden. During that period, the seriousness of the macroeconomic imbalances was recognized, and drastic adjustment and stabilization measures were taken. These prepared the ground for the most

Table 4 Selected economic and social indicators, Denmark, 1913–92

| | Average annual growth in real GDP per capita (%) | | | Average annual growth in labour productivity (GDP per hour worked), (%) | | | GDP per capita (1990 international dollars) | | |
|---|---|---|---|---|---|---|---|---|---|
| | 1913–50 | 1950–73 | 1973–92 | 1913–50 | 1950–73 | 1973–92 | 1913 | 1950 | 1992 |
| Denmark | 1.6 | 3.1 | 1.6 | 1.5 | 4.5 | 1.7 | 3 764 | 6 683 | 18 293 |
| Germany[b] | 0.3 | 5 | 2.1 | 0.6 | 6 | 2.7 | 3 833 | 4 281 | 19 351 |
| Sweden | 2.1 | 3.1 | 1.2 | 2.8 | 4.1 | 1.3 | 3 096 | 6 738 | 16 927 |
| Western Europe[c] | 1.2 | 3.8 | 1.8 | 1.8 | 4.7 | 2.3 | 3 482 | 5 513 | 17 412 |
| United States | 1.6 | 2.4 | 1.4 | 2.5 | 2.7 | 1.1 | 5 307 | 9 573 | 21 558 |

| | Unemployment, average rate (%) | | | Consumer price index, period average (%) | | | Life expectancy (years) | |
|---|---|---|---|---|---|---|---|---|
| | 1950–73 | 1974–83 | 1984–93 | 1950–73 | 1974–83 | 1984–93 | 1960 | 1998 |
| Denmark | 2.6 | 7.6 | 7.8[a] | 4.8 | 10.7 | 3.7 | 72.2 | 75.8 |
| Germany[b] | 2.5 | 4.1 | 6.2 | 2.7 | 4.9 | 2.3 | 69.5 | 76.7 |
| Sweden | 1.8 | 2.3 | 3.2 | 4.7 | 10.2 | 6.3 | 73.2 | 79.2 |
| Western Europe[c] | 2.4 | 4.9 | 6.8 | 4.2 | 9.4 | 4 | | |
| United States | 4.6 | 7.4 | 6.4 | 2.7 | 8.2 | 3.8 | 69.8 | 76.5 |

[a] 1984–92.
[b] Refers to territory within the boundaries of the former Federal Republic of Germany.
[c] 12-country average.

Sources: Maddison, 1995; World Bank, 2000.

Figure 17   Unemployment rate in Denmark, 1960–2000

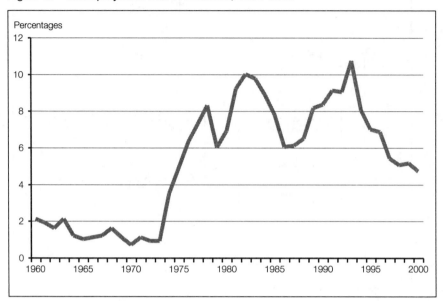

Source: OECD, 2000b; ILO, 2002.

recent period, in which Denmark experienced a fast and strong recovery, with annual rates of growth of output of 3.5 per cent from 1994 to 2000, of labour productivity of 2.4 per cent, and of employment of 1.1 per cent. The proportion of long-term unemployed fell from 32.1 per cent in 1994 to 20.5 per cent in 1999 (ILO, 2002).

## A summary assessment

The indicators and ratings reviewed above – including the core indicators compiled in table 3 – yield the conclusion that Denmark currently ranks high in terms of both social and economic performance. On many of the decent work indicators selected, the country is at or near the top of the scale of members of the European Union and the Organisation for Economic Co-operation and Development.

Denmark has high levels of labour market participation and employment. At nearly 77 per cent, the proportion of employed persons in the Danish population of working age is the highest in Europe, and the second-highest in the OECD. Nowhere else in the industrialized world are there fewer inactive people aged 25–54 years, showing that relatively few Danes are either excluded from work for economic reasons or prefer not to work. The high employment levels and the low inactivity rates apply to men as well as women, and to young people 15–24 years of age.

The Danish unemployment rate was less than 5 per cent in 2001. This level is comparable to that of the United States, and much lower than the averages for Europe and the industrialized world as a whole. Nevertheless, a few countries have managed to lower unemployment rates further. Many new jobs were generated in Denmark in the latter half of the 1990s, bringing down the proportion of unemployed people from 10.7 per cent in 1993 to 4.7 per cent in 2000.

Comparatively few people in Denmark are out of work for a long time. However, the unemployment rate among immigrants, especially those from developing countries, remains relatively high, although this group has also benefited from the overall drop in unemployment.

The number of hours worked, per week and per year, is low in Denmark. This may be interpreted as a collective preference for a certain way of life, with more time for social, family and leisure activities.

The Danish population is among the most educated, measured in terms of years of schooling, and among the best trained in terms of labour market skills. Free access to education is a major means of moving towards equality of opportunity for all.

Occupational health has reached a high level, measured in terms of standard indicators of safety and occupational disease. Accident rates are comparatively low. However, the prevalence of stress and mental disorders is reported to be rising quickly, in Denmark and other Nordic countries, as a result of changing working conditions (e.g. working intensity and tempo, high performance demands), expansion of information technology, and possibly also ageing of the working population. "Well-being at work" has become a major issue (Nordic Council, 2000).

The Danish population is well protected against social contingencies and labour market risks, including unemployment, disability, sickness, maternity and old age. Income protection is especially high for the unemployed, who benefit from relatively high replacement rates for a longer period than in any other country. Danish workers, however, fare less well than the average European when it comes to employment protection, such as notice periods and severance pay.

Denmark is among the most egalitarian countries in the world, as indicated by the comparatively high degree of income equality. The main reasons for this equality are the relatively low wage dispersion and the high minimum wage (negotiated in collective agreements but used as a reference throughout the economy) and the redistributive effects of extensive social transfers. Because of the wage and income equality and the high employment levels, there is little poverty in Denmark by international standards. Income equality also tends to support gender equality.

As regards gender equality, Denmark and Sweden score high marks. In the two countries, women have reached a relatively high level of education and employment. The gaps between women and men with regard to labour force participation, employment and unemployment levels have shrunk. Women have made great advances in the labour market, especially through opportunities in the public sector and in social services. They have been less successful in accessing certain other sectors and occupations, or higher-level managerial, technical and professional positions. This is reflected in persistent horizontal and vertical labour market segregation. Also, in both absolute and relative terms, there are few women entrepreneurs in Denmark. Hence, while Denmark has made progress towards greater gender equality, there is room for improvement in terms of access to some occupations and in breaking through the "glass ceiling" barring the way to high-paid managerial and professional jobs, especially in the private sector. The occupational segregation observed may in part reflect educational choices and cultural patterns rather than workplace discrimination.

Denmark has ratified all the fundamental International Labour Conventions. Barring some instances of government intervention in collective bargaining rounds in the 1980s and 1990s, which became subject to scrutiny by the ILO Governing Body Committee on Freedom of Association, fundamental worker rights are generally respected in Denmark. Forced and child labour do not exist. With regard to discrimination in employment and occupation, the Government actively monitors its labour market policies and practices in order to adopt remedial measures when needed. In the 2000 bargaining round, LO and DA agreed to investigate and monitor more closely issues of equality and non-discrimination.

Collective bargaining is highly developed. Together with Sweden and Finland, Denmark has the most comprehensive collective organization of the labour market. The large majority of workers and employers are organized in trade unions and employer associations. The majority of workers are covered by collective agreements. Collective bargaining on wages and other terms of employment and working conditions plays a prominent role in Denmark. Furthermore, on a large number of social and economic policy issues, Denmark stands out in practising social dialogue through consultation and negotiation between the Government and workers' and employers' organizations at various levels (see Chapter 2). The level and quality of social participation are high.

Denmark's high social standards are to a large degree matched by the country's economic performance. Economic growth accelerated during the 1990s, turning Denmark into the second most prosperous country in the

European Union and the fifth richest in the OECD in terms of GDP per capita. This is remarkable for a small country with no natural resources, a small average size of enterprise, and limited scope for economies of scale in production. The last factor may explain why Denmark is below the average for Europe in terms of productivity per employed person (5.5 per cent below the average in 1998), although – in view of the relatively low number of hours worked – hourly productivity is average. Obviously, Denmark's high rank on the prosperity scale is related to its high employment and, presumably, to its high level of social transfers. As these are largely financed through taxes, Denmark's taxes are among the highest, notably on income.

In summary, Denmark today displays many signs of decent work, scoring high on almost all the indicators used above. It is the "universality" of decency across policy areas that distinguishes the country from many others, including the United States, which ranks high on some indicators, but lags behind in other respects.

This assessment of working conditions in Denmark is largely consistent with the findings of the European Community Household Panel 1994–96. The data showed, inter alia, that – together with Belgium, the Netherlands and Finland – Denmark had relatively low proportions of dead-end jobs and low-pay/low-productivity jobs, and moreover, that Denmark had the largest share of "good jobs", defined as those with good pay, good job security, employer-provided training and career prospects (European Commission, 2001). On the other hand, the present assessment is not consistent with the ranking given to Denmark by the United Nations Development Programme (UNDP) on its human development index (HDI). In both 2000 and 2001, the country was positioned only in fifteenth place according to this index (UNDP, 2001). There are several reasons why Denmark fares less well on this index than in our evaluation. The HDI is a composite index based on three factors: longevity, as measured by life expectancy at birth; educational attainment, as measured by a combination of adult literacy and the combined gross primary, secondary and tertiary enrolment ratio; and standard of living, as measured by GDP per capita at purchasing power parity. As such, it is much less comprehensive than the range of social indicators used in this book. It relies solely on general education and neglects vocational education and training. Finally, life expectancy, which in Denmark is almost two years less than in other European countries, has a relatively high weight in the HDI. From the perspective of decent work, Denmark's relatively low life expectancy would matter only if it were work related. There is evidence, however, that it is primarily a result of general lifestyle and dietary habits. The low life expectancy also seems to be at odds with survey findings indicating that Denmark ranks highest among all the European Union countries in terms of satisfaction of the people with their own health and with life in general (Eurostat, 2001). In 2000, 57 per cent of all adult Danes, and 61 per cent of women, reported that they were "very satisfied" with their life in general. The EU-15 average was 17 per cent. Adding those who were "fairly satisfied" brings the total proportion of satisfied people up to 95 per cent, compared with 77 per cent in the EU-15.

# HOW DENMARK HAS ATTAINED DECENT WORK: INSTITUTIONS AND POLICIES

2

As outlined in Chapter 1, by the end of the 1990s Denmark had reached an impressive record of decent work that few countries could match. Although certain deficits remain and new challenges continue to emerge, on the whole, working and living conditions may be rated among the best in the world.

In this chapter we analyse why and how the country has attained its decent work status. We look at the social institutions, i.e. the policies and actors that have given shape to Denmark's social architecture. We will demonstrate a significant inter-action of different policies producing a high degree of consistency and coherence in the overall policy framework. Social scientists would speak of a "system". But it would be wrong to think that this system is the outcome of a predesigned strategy, devised in one ingenious stroke. Far from it, what we see today in Denmark is the result of a long process of policy formation, which proceeded in piecemeal fashion to solve one problem after another. If there is any ingenuity in the system, it resides in the consultations and negotiations between the main actors: the government at local, regional and central levels, and the workers and employers and their representative collective organizations. The concertation manifests itself in the mode and style in which the parties act together to address and resolve the issues they confront. There is extensive political mobilization and activation and many people are involved in discussing and deciding about social issues.

There is a long history behind the way in which the Danes tackle their social problems. At times, there has been conflict and confrontation between the parties, but gradually, relations evolved in line with commonly defined and accepted prin-ciples and rules that underlie a culture of dialogue, negotiation and compromise.

## Basic institutional features

Denmark had a population of 5.3 million and a labour force of 2.9 million in 2000. Together with Finland, Iceland, Norway and Sweden, it belongs to the

Nordic group of countries, best known as welfare states. Here, this refers to a high standard of living with a combination of relatively high levels of GDP per capita, low unemployment, large welfare entitlements and high rates of labour force participation. Additionally, low inequality in income and high social equality, a large public sector and strong social partners, reflected in high union membership rates and extensive collective bargaining, are also associated with welfare states. All these characterizations fit Denmark as well as the other Nordic countries, but nevertheless large differences exist among these countries. Their recent history, particularly with regard to membership of the European Union (EU) and the European Monetary Union (EMU), illustrates some of these differences (Norway having chosen to stay out of both, Finland being a member of both, and Sweden and Denmark members of the EU but not of the EMU).

The welfare state model came under growing strain, particularly in the first half of the 1990s when most of the Nordic countries experienced an economic crisis with high rates of inflation, large fiscal deficits and high unemployment. This led many authors to suggest that this particular strand of modern economic growth had reached its limits (Stephens, 1996). The main argument was that these economies had become uncompetitive because of high welfare expenditure at a time when markets were rapidly globalizing and when cost competition was more intense than ever.

The latter half of the 1990s showed the remarkable resilience of the welfare state model, particularly in Denmark. The principles and entitlements associated with the welfare state have, in fact, provided much of the adaptive capacity and resources required to move rapidly out of the recession and onto a renewed high and balanced growth path with a sharp fall in unemployment. In no way has this implied resistance to change. In the area of labour market policy particularly, many changes have been introduced and possibly more will be required as the effect of long-term demographic change inexorably bears upon the ratio of the active to the inactive population. However, the many policy changes agreed upon have not turned away from the basic welfare principles that secured the growth, wealth and social cohesion of Denmark for the better part of the twentieth century. A better understanding of the functioning of the Danish economy and society, particularly as it moved out of severe crisis in 1993 and onto a higher growth path, on the basis of its welfare principles and benefits rather than against them, would provide an important input to the discussion on growth paths, given the importance currently accorded to competitive gains based on reducing costs, in particular labour costs.

The theme of institutions is increasingly recognized as an important dimension of economic growth and development. Institutions, in the sense of humanly devised rules as defined by Douglas North (1990) that structure political, economic and social interactions, whether formal or informal, reduce transaction and information costs and facilitate the shaping of agreements and policies among actors. This is especially the case for labour market institutions which some see as determining growth and development. Such institutions, both formal and informal, and normative rather than legal, form an essential part of Denmark's overall performance.

At the core of the Danish model lie some basic institutional features. Among the more salient are:

- A high degree of political and economic decentralization. In addition to the central state administration, there are at the regional level 14 counties plus the metropolitan areas of Copenhagen and Frederiksberg, and at the local level 273 municipal authorities, each with extensive responsibilities and powers. The counties and municipalities administer approximately 33 per cent of the gross national budget and employ almost 75 per cent of all public servants.
- An economy based largely on small and medium-sized enterprises. Firms with nine or fewer employees account for over 90 per cent of all firms, and firms with up to 49 employees represent 52.5 per cent of total employment (OECD, 2000d).
- An open economy (exports and imports are each equivalent to about 30 per cent of GDP).
- A homogeneous and egalitarian society (with among the smallest differences between the first and last income quintiles).
- An active society in terms of participation in social, cultural and political activities. While in the EU-15, slightly less than 50 per cent of citizens took part in such activities in 1998, the rate for Denmark and Sweden was around 85 per cent (Eurostat and European Commission, 2001).

In spite of its extensive public sector (37.6 per cent of all employees in 1999), its welfare entitlements and the ubiquitous presence of social partners, Denmark has been and still is far removed from a traditional centralized state. In fact, the defining characteristic of the Danish model, in addition to its strong attachment to basic democratic freedoms and principles, is the remarkable flexibility of economic and social organization. Such flexibility is not normally associated with welfare states, yet it is pervasive in Denmark, within its legal tradition, the organization of firms and the labour market. It is based on dialogue, mutual trust and cooperation stemming from shared basic values – precisely those values that define the Danish way. This tradition has its roots in the strong cooperative movements in agriculture, and in the crafts and guilds that started to forge industrialization in the latter half of the nineteenth century.

It stems from the tradition for self-reliance of small agricultural communities, and the popular high school movement which took shape at about the same time. But it has been reinvented several times as new challenges and situations have emerged.

The success of small firms in Denmark owes much to the tradition of cooperation among them, as well as to the shaping of local private and public support systems, whether in the area of product and technology development, export promotion, credit financing, training of the workforce, or social and labour market security. Such cooperation is perhaps best exemplified in the extensive consultations and negotiations among employers' and workers' organizations. Many owners of small and large firms have previously been wage earners and members of a union.

Collective labour market organization and collective agreements have often been misinterpreted as cartels, and as a major cause of inefficiency and suboptimal allocation of resources. Far from introducing rigidities and costs, social dialogue is in fact a source of remarkable flexibility as well as stability. The social partners in Denmark have a distinct preference for reaching their own agreements and for limiting government interference in areas of their own competence. Such autonomy of action represents a clear alternative to other regimes of governance, such as the state (bureaucracy) or the market. Bargaining between associations can significantly increase the range of strategic options for solving public policy problems (Streeck and Schmitter, 1985).

The preference in Denmark for collective bargaining can explain why agree--ment among the social partners has at times been preferred to ratification of an ILO Convention through an act of Parliament, even though the standard is the same and its application regularly reviewed by employers and workers. This does not exclude serious differences of opinion and periods of conflict, as most recently in 1998 when collective negotiations broke down and the Government decided to intervene. But such crises have not altered the basic faith in social dialogue that constitutes a pillar of the Danish model and a feature of its social and economic achievements.

Denmark is a lively democracy that works to put into practice the basic rights associated with a democratic regime. The political, social and economic rights expounded in the Universal Declaration of Human Rights are exercised in Denmark, through direct and indirect participation of citizens in myriad associations and organizations that can affect political, economic and social decisions. This reinforces the exercise of democracy in a context of high living standards and low inequality – all things that go together in Denmark.

In the following sections, we analyse the institutional framework through a more detailed account of the key actors and policies.

# Social and economic policies

## Collective bargaining and social dialogue

The high level of organization of employers and workers in Denmark, as well as the forms of collaboration through consultations and bargaining, have been well described by Visser (2001). The Danish pattern of industrial relations falls within the corporatist model, with extensive consultations and negotiations taking place between highly representative social partners, and with little state intervention. The specific pattern prevailing in Denmark has been termed "associative corporatism" (Amin and Thomas, 1996, quoted in Visser, 2001) or "negotiated economy" (Jessop, Nielsen and Pedersen, 1993, quoted in Visser, 2001).

### Principal characteristics

The principal characteristics of industrial relations in Denmark are:

- a high level of union membership and representation for both employers and workers;
- decentralization of decision-making within a framework agreed at the central level;
- the role of the State limited to that of facilitator;
- intensive consultations through formal and informal networks at various levels as a basis for consensus and agreement building.

The first characteristic can be readily verified by the density rates of employers' organizations and trade unions. At the central level, the biggest confederation of employers – the Danish Employers' Confederation (DA) – covers around 640,000 wage earners and coordinates collective bargaining strategies, while its member organizations control collective bargaining at industry and enterprise levels. Employers in the financial sector, agriculture and the public sector have their own associations outside the DA. On the trade union side, the Danish Confederation of Trade Unions (LO) is composed of 20 national trade union affiliates and six cartels of trade unions, with a total membership of 1.5 million workers. The LO is an influential coordinating body, which acts on behalf of the trade union movement in relation to the DA and to the public service. The Confederation of White-Collar and Crown Servants (FTF), with a membership of 323,000, represents public servants. The Danish Confederation of Graduate Employee Associations (AC) has members in both public and private sectors. Both employers and workers are organized at the local, regional and central levels. While employers are organized in associations according to industry, trade unions are organized by trade or craft.

The second characteristic – decentralized decision-making – is unique to Denmark. Nordic welfare states tend to be associated with centralized collective bargaining, and this was the case in Denmark up to the mid-1980s. The economic crisis of the 1970s showed for the first time the limitations of the centralized collective bargaining system: major conflicts between the social partners could not be avoided, and the failure of the parties to settle their disputes provoked state intervention in three bargaining rounds. As a result, the parties decided to move towards a decentralized coordinated collective bargaining system. This move marked the end of a particular pattern of wage negotiations, with high nominal wage adjustments and fixed across-the-board compensation for consumer price increases, which had led to considerable wage drift. Indexation clauses and centralized negotiations between DA and LO, aimed at improving the lowest wages by narrowing the gap with the average wage, contributed to such drift. Formal indexation of wages was ended in 1982. Employers' organizations pressed for more decentralized negotiations and workers recognized that high unemployment might be related to high nominal wage increases and high inflation. A new pattern, based on wage and price stability and high levels of employment, with more decentralized negotiations has since been adopted.

The role of the State as a facilitator, fully respecting the autonomy and responsibility of the social partners, has been a constant policy in Denmark, except in times of crisis when the parties could not reach agreement and the Government felt obliged to intervene. This was particularly the case in sensitive sectors, such as hospitals, meat packaging and slaughterhouses, and in prolonged conflicts. This pattern was more common in the 1970s, although it recurred in 1985 and 1998. The State is present in technical consultations between the social partners before the formal bargaining takes place, at which economic and social data are jointly reviewed and indicative figures for levels of wage increases, compatible with other macroeconomic variables, including economic growth, price stability and competitiveness, are considered. Lind (2000) notes that the outcome of the bargaining round is often close to the level envisaged by the Government in its initial views.

Consultation, cooperation and negotiation among social partners are pervasive in Denmark. Typical areas for collective bargaining are wages, pensions, supplementary social benefits and working time. Other areas, such as productivity, work organization, occupational safety and health, training and education, labour market policy and unemployment benefits, are addressed through consultation and cooperation at enterprise, local and national levels.

Collective bargaining takes place at various levels. The first bargaining rounds are at the central level, followed by rounds at the local level. Until 2000, bargaining rounds were organized every two years, with rare exceptions. During the 2000 bargaining round, the parties (in the DA/LO area only) decided to extend the duration of collective agreements to four years, in order to reach socially acceptable trade-offs at the various bargaining levels.

In addition to negotiating collective agreements on pay and working time, workers can voice their concerns on other issues and influence the decision-making process within the enterprises in which they are employed through various mechanisms. The shop steward system is the oldest one and dates back to 1900, but it was really after the Second World War that greater cooperation between workers and management was promoted and given a new impetus. Workplace democracy was considered to be an efficient means of restoring national competitiveness and increasing job satisfaction. By way of collective agreements, cooperation committees were established to organize the dialogue between the parties at the workplace. These committees have since evolved to take on two sets of responsibilities: information; and codetermination of the principles guiding issues such as restructuring, working conditions, personnel policies, work organization, new technology and training. There are various other structures through which workers' participation in decision-making in enterprises is promoted, some of which, such as the safety committee group, were established by law.

Consultation of employers and workers is also institutionalized at the local, regional and national levels, through committees advising on issues such as occupational safety and health, work environment, and occupational and vocational training. Employers and workers have majority seating on the boards of local secondary schools that provide vocational training programmes, in order to ensure close links with the local labour market and evolving demands for skills, which are key to sustaining the Danish apprenticeship scheme. Employers and workers also sit on a number of national committees (labour market policies, occupational safety and health, social policy, vocational education), reviewing and advising on policies, economic development, and labour costs and competitiveness in Denmark and abroad.

## Historical evolution

The tradition of mutual trust and dialogue between the social partners, notwithstanding their conflicting interests, dates back to 1899 when the so-called September Compromise ended one of the biggest industrial disputes to date. The September Compromise was the first basic agreement concluded and it spelled out basic rights and obligations that still form the basis of the collective bargaining system:

- the right to organize;
- the employer's right to manage and control the work;
- the right to take industrial action; and
- the peace obligation (which precludes strike action during the period of a collective agreement).

The September Compromise marked the beginning of an institutional approach to conflict resolution, as the parties moved from a decentralized industrial conflict strategy to a centralized and institutionalized negotiating relationship. The social partners recognized the need for an overall institutional framework to govern their relations and guide their incipient organizations (established in 1897 and 1898). The centralization of the collective bargaining system was then a major objective of the DA in order to reduce the number of conflicts at the enterprise level through the peace obligation. As this system of collective bargaining proved efficient, the main source of labour law was collective agreements and the State's role remained confined to that of facilitator. By comparison, in Sweden, it was not until 1938 that a basic agreement, with rules on the settlement of disputes, was concluded; this has meant that far more legislation has been passed in Sweden than in Denmark. As mentioned earlier, this system of collective bargaining has survived till now, although in the 1980s the social partners decided on a strategic shift toward a decentralized but coordinated system.

Nowadays, the top organizations coordinate bargaining over pay and working time and fix the bargaining calendar in a given industry. Bargaining at the local level takes place within the parameters set by *framework agreements* signed by the top organizations at industry or branch levels. With the *Climate Agreement* concluded in 1999, the LO and the DA agreed to develop a common understanding of the economically acceptable level of pay increase and to come up with joint estimates. This agreement proved useful in ensuring better coordination of the decentralized bargaining, as well as more realistic expectations. It can also be noted that any LO/DA agreement, especially on wage adjustments, sets the trend for both the non-covered private sector (50 per cent) and the public sector.

### Wage bargaining

It is in the area of wage bargaining that the pattern of industrial relations is perhaps most refined. The social partners like to see it as a decentralized system of wage bargaining, prepared for and accompanied by a sophisticated system of information sharing, prior consultations and shared bargaining principles, such as on the economic variables to be taken into account in any particular round of negotiation, as for instance wage increases in competitor countries. Scholars see it more as "centralized decentralization" (Madsen, Jorgensen and Due, 2000) as it fits neither the centralized nor the decentralized collective bargaining model. In fact, there is a division of labour: the member organizations of the LO and the DA, by negotiating minimum wage rates at the sectoral and branch levels, set guidelines for wage bargaining at the local level which takes place once a year. The local negotiators take the guidelines into account, but adjust pay in line with the profitability and other economic circumstances of the enterprise. Wage settlements in the bargaining area of the DA and the LO cover more than 40 per cent of private sector employees. So-called adhesion agreements for non-covered segments of the private sector bring the coverage up to 50 per cent. In addition, collective agreements in the public sector include a provision linking wages to those in the private sector. In the end, a wage structure emerges that reflects both general and specific economic considerations.

Recent analysis of collective bargaining is revisiting the well-known arguments on the superior economic performance of either centralized or decentralized structures (the hump-shape hypothesis of Calmfors and Driffill (1993)) in favour of an optimum combination of horizontal and vertical coordination. This combination is not associated with any one particular formal mode of collective bargaining, but rather with a series of modes that ensure effective economy-wide coordination within a formally decentralized bargaining framework (Traxler and Kittel, 2000). This pattern fits rather well the Danish practice in so far as wage bargaining is formally decentralized to the level of the individual firm or industry, and even within firms, to workers or groups of workers. However, there is undeniably a high level of coordination in that all negotiators have access to the same information, share basic principles established in framework agreements, and tend to negotiate outcomes that are remarkably similar. Standardization of wage adjustments is also fostered by consideration of labour cost data and price movements in Denmark and abroad, as mapped out by the Tripartite Statistics Committee (comprising the DA, the LO and central Government), with a view to ensuring that international competitiveness is taken into account in wage negotiations.

Comparing the two periods 1986–92 and 1993–99, the rate of annual increase in real hourly earnings in industry in Denmark dropped marginally by 0.3 percentage points, with a significant decline in Germany and a sharp increase in Sweden (table 5). The rate of growth in the latter period was lower in Denmark than in Sweden and only slightly higher than in Germany. However, because of lower growth in industrial productivity in Denmark, unit labour costs increased faster in Denmark then in the other two countries (figures given here are for the total economy and hence not strictly comparable). The rate of increase of unit labour costs nevertheless declined sharply between the two periods.

The earnings data in table 5 refer only to industry. Wage adjustments in other sectors of the economy have a varied pattern, as they respond to both overall economic trends and sector-specific dynamics. Table 6 provides data on real wage adjustments over the period 1996–98, together with the proportion of

Table 5    Average annual percentage change in wages, productivity and income
in Denmark, Germany and Sweden, 1986–92 and 1993–99

|  | 1986–92 | | | 1993–99 | | |
|---|---|---|---|---|---|---|
|  | Denmark | Germany[a] | Sweden | Denmark | Germany[a] | Sweden |
| Real value added per person employed (industry) | 0.06 | 1.82 | 2.29 | 1.27 | 1.56 | 5.62 |
| Real hourly earnings (industry) | 1.86 | 2.34 | 0.90 | 1.56 | 1.21 | 2.35 |
| Unit labour costs (total economy) | 4.64 | 2.47 | 6.62 | 1.43 | 0.79 | 1.17 |
| Real GDP per capita | 1.01 | 2.24 | 0.71 | 2.13 | 0.98 | 2.00 |

[a] Data for the period before 1991 refer to the Federal Republic of Germany; data for the period after 1991 to Germany.

Source: OECD, 2000a.

Table 6    Change in real wages by economic activity in Denmark, 1996–98

|  | Percentage change in real wages | | | | Percentage of women in the workforce |
|---|---|---|---|---|---|
|  | 1996 | 1997 | 1998 | 1996–98 |  |
| Manufacturing | 4.80 | 0.09 | 2.49 | 2.44 | 31.3 |
| Construction | 3.71 | −1.21 | 2.85 | 1.76 | 10.6 |
| Wholesale and retail trade | 3.00 | −3.16 | 2.46 | 0.73 | 44.0 |
| Financial intermediation | 1.76 | −0.22 | 2.86 | 1.46 | 52.4 |
| Education | −3.34 | −0.58 | 2.61 | −0.47 | 59.1 |
| Health and social work | −2.02 | −2.83 | 4.97 | −0.02 | 85.3 |

Source: Yearbook of Labour Statistics, ILO (2001) and IMF (2000) (CPI index).

women in employment. The two sectors in which women are in a majority are also those where employment is mostly in the public sector, and where real wages declined. The data do not allow any link to be established between the proportion of women in the workforce and wage trends.

Nominal wage restraint has become a defining feature of collective bargaining in Denmark, with a focus on wage increases compatible with stable inflation and high growth. This is evident from the wage settlements over the past three decades. The data show a clear shift in the bargaining strategy, resulting in a convergence of the rates of nominal and real wage growth. Nominal wages in Denmark grew at an average annual rate of 14.2 per cent in the 1970s, 6.5 per cent in the 1980s and 3.7 per cent from 1990 to 1998. Real wages increased by 3.3 per cent, 0.7 per cent and 1.7 per cent respectively. This means that in the 1990s workers secured higher real wage increases than in the 1980s, although nominal wage growth in the 1980s was much higher. Moreover, both nominal and real wage growth were extremely volatile in the 1970s, and more stable in the 1980s and especially in the 1990s. This is reflected in the standard deviations of annual growth rates, which were 4.38 in the 1970s, 2.21 in the 1980s and 0.90 in the 1990s for nominal wage changes, and 3.39, 2.14 and 0.54 for real wage growth (calculated from OECD, 2000a).

This shift implies that wage bargaining has taken into account the macro-economic determinants of microeconomic decisions regarding wage increases and inflation, including working time (both annual working time which includes leave and weekly working time) and productivity based on work organization, training, use of new technology and pay-related productivity incentives. There is evidence that such parameters have indeed cropped up in the negotiating agenda at all levels, in the private as well as in the public sector. In addition, the duration of collective bargaining agreements was extended to four years as from 2000 (in the DA/LO area only), with safeguards should price inflation turn out to be different than forecast. The inability of both employers and workers to conclude negotiations in 1998 and the subsequent intervention of the Government illustrated the difficulty of such negotiations and the impossibility for negotiators to strike an agreement that is not supported by the rank and file membership. However, wage restraint has been a characteristic of wage negotiations in Denmark during the latter half of the 1990s and early years of the 2000s. This should be interpreted as nominal wage increases in line with increases observed in the main trading countries, compatible with stable inflation as well as with other aspirations such as more annual leave (with the introduction of five additional days of leave to be granted on a flexible basis), and the actuarial viability of labour market pensions. The most recent wage data available indicate that the principle of wage restraint may have been weakened, in particular by the bargaining coordination mechanisms (Denmark: Collective bargaining system is out of step, EIROnline).

## Coverage of collective agreements

As mentioned earlier, the long-standing and efficient tradition of collective bargaining in Denmark results in the formation of rules of law being entrusted first to the parties of the labour market through collective agreements and, secondly, to the Labour Court and Arbitration Boards through establishment of case law. Legislation has been enacted only to protect certain categories of workers whose organizations failed to protect them, or when the parties failed to reach an agreement (Jacobsen and Hasselbach, 1998). This in turn means that international and regional instruments regulating labour market matters are implemented first and foremost through collective agreements in Denmark. There is an ongoing debate on whether all employees therefore enjoy the protection provided by those instruments. The European Commission posed this question to the Danish Ministry of Labour in November 1999 in relation to the implementation of the 1993 Directive on Working Time, generating a debate in Denmark about the coverage of collective agreements. Possibly 1 million workers are not covered by collective agreements (Madsen, 2000). Figures for direct coverage of collective bargaining in Denmark vary from 60 per cent to 85 per cent of employees. As a result of pressure from the European Commission, the LO and the DA improved the procedure concerning the implementation of EU Directives and concluded an agreement on the implementation of the Working Time Directive, effective from February 2000. The agreement applies to all employees within the LO/DA field who are not covered by collective agreements, and to both organized and unorganized employees. In addition, the DA sent out a communication indicating that all employees in DA-affiliated enterprises, not covered by a collective agreement, would nevertheless benefit from the provisions of the Directive. Finally, the LO, the DA and the Government expressed their political will to settle any pending matter in relation to the regulation of working time.

More recently, in June 2001, the Parliament adopted a law to transpose the EU Directive on Part-Time work. The law essentially extends an existing LO/DA agreement to areas not covered by the agreement. This new method of implementation has been contested by those employers' and workers' organizations that have been bypassed, and by all of them for not having being consulted (Jorgensen, 2001). It is nevertheless too early to tell whether Denmark has moved towards a combined (statutory and agreement-based) implementation of EU Directives.

The legislation-based regulation pursued by the EU challenges the Danish model, and may tilt the balance between the forms of labour market regulation in favour of legislation.

## Occupational safety and health

Policies and practices in occupational safety and health (OSH) reflect the basic hallmarks of Danish social policy in general. First, while they provide adequate rehabilitation and financial compensation for workers who have accidents or occupational diseases, the basic thrust of policy is directed to prevention rather than compensation. Second, a closely knit public institutional framework has been established to implement the OSH policy. Third, employers and workers and their collective organizations have been closely, and increasingly, involved in the design and implementation of the policy.

The legislative base for the OSH policy is the Working Environment Act of 1975, which has been amended several times. It covers all dependent employees and self-employed persons. The aim of the Act is to create a safe and healthy working environment in accordance with technical and social developments. The focus is on prevention, guidance and planning of safety and health at work, as well as long-term hazards, the pace of work and psychosocial factors. Provisions of the Working Environment Act cover the safety and health activities of enterprises; duties of employers, supervisors, employees, suppliers, project managers and advisers; the performance of work; the design of the workplace; technical equipment, substances and materials; rest periods and rest days; special provisions for people under the age of 18 years; medical examinations; and institutions for counselling and execution of OSH policy.

The institutional setting for OSH policy comprises the following:

- The Working Environment Authority responsible for implementing the Working Environment Act under the overall responsibility of the Ministry of Labour. It monitors compliance with the law and regulations through inspection, and provides guidance to enterprises and their safety organizations to enable them to ensure a safe work environment.
- The tripartite Working Environment Council, which advises the Government on the drafting of new regulations and action on occupational safety and heath.
- The tripartite Sector Safety Councils, established in 1997 to strengthen the role and responsibility of the social partners, inter alia through information, counselling, education and training in sectoral and enterprise policies and measures of OSH.
- The National Institute of Occupational Health, which conducts research.
- The Working Environment Appeal Board, which oversees decisions made by the Working Environment Authority.
- The Occupational Health Service (OHS), which acts as an intermediary between the regulation of the working environment and the application of measures in the enterprises. Occupational health services are provided by private companies, which offer guidance and assistance to enterprises and their employees on safety and health at work.

During the 1990s, the Government took a number of initiatives to improve safety and health conditions in Denmark. Among them was an action plan, launched in 1996, for a "Clean Working Environment 2005"; this specified objectives in the field of safety and health aimed at reducing the incidence of occupational accidents and diseases, together with an action plan for the period 1994–2000 which would reduce by 50 per cent the incidence of occupational injuries resulting from monotonous and repetitive work.

The social partners play an influential role in OSH policy and administration. Already in the nineteenth century there was debate about how safety and health at work could be promoted through collective bargaining rather than through legislation. Most recently, the role of the social partners has been further strengthened through the Sector Safety Councils and through increased involvement in the Working Environment Council. It is believed that worker and employer involvement in the design of OSH policy and measures is essential for greater legitimacy and better results.

## Social security and welfare

Denmark, like other Nordic countries, has developed an extensive system of social protection for the economically active and non-active populations. In principle, all citizens have the right to income transfers and social services.

Incomes are redistributed through taxes, transfers and subsidies to almost everybody. Benefits include unemployment benefits, old-age pensions, anticipatory pensions and early retirement leave, sickness benefits, disability benefits, maternity benefits, social assistance and a variety of other entitlements, such as benefits for children and students, and housing allowances. Extensive care services have been developed largely as a response to ageing, and changing family structures and employment patterns. They comprise cost-free and subsidized health care, day care, care for dependent elderly persons, and rehabilitation. Targeted measures are available for particular groups, including people with physical and mental disabilities, groups that are socially excluded or at risk of social exclusion, people who are mentally ill, and suffering from drug and alcohol dependency (for a good discussion of the Nordic welfare states and their modernization, see Palme, 1999, and Kiander, 2001).

Social protection as a citizen's right, universalism and inclusion are fundamental principles of the Danish welfare system: all citizens have equal rights to social security benefits and social services. The underlying idea is to promote equality at a high level, rather than equality in meeting minimum needs. Moreover, benefits and care services span the entire life of citizens "from cradle to grave". However, social policy is closely linked to labour market policy. All beneficiaries are subject to criteria of employability and availability for work. For instance, participation in active labour market programmes is a condition for receiving cash social assistance and unemployment benefits. Such inclusiveness contrasts with other protection systems outside the Nordic countries. In several English-speaking countries, only a low level of public social security is provided, the coverage is limited to low-income groups and assistance is often means-tested. Citizens with moderate or high incomes are largely expected to organize their security and services privately. The continental European countries have complemented the basic social security by a system of social insurance, which in the case of unemployment, disability or old age provides benefits linked to previous earnings. Yet, this system does not cover as much of the population as in the Nordic countries. Also, these countries emphasize the role of the family and the principle of "subsidiarity", meaning that the State should interfere only if the family is unable to care adequately for its members. For this reason, the great majority of benefits are oriented to preserving the traditional household, excluding non-working wives from independent rights to social security, and encouraging motherhood without developing day care and similar family services (Esping-Andersen, 1990).

In Denmark and the other Nordic countries, the public sector is primarily responsible for providing benefits and services. Improved services for children, the elderly and disabled persons are designed to reconcile and connect work with family life. The planning and delivery of social services are decentralized, with local government taking charge of administering the social sector.

### Costs and financing of social protection

In 1997, total **gross social expenditure** in Denmark amounted to 32.0 per cent of GDP. This was the second-highest level of social spending in the OECD after Sweden (34.8 per cent). The rate for the United States was 22.9 per cent. About 32 per cent of the social expenditure in Denmark was on services (payments in kind), and about 65 per cent on transfer payments. Social security spending made up 52.5 per cent of total public spending.

**Gross public social expenditure** in Denmark was 30.7 per cent of GDP in 1997, again the second-highest rate in the OECD after Sweden (31.8 per cent). Of the public social outlays in Denmark, 7.0 per cent went to old-age and survivors' pensions, 2.0 per cent to disability spending, 0.7 per cent to sickness benefits, 3.8 per cent to unemployment benefits and 6.8 per cent to health. **Gross voluntary private expenditure** reached 0.9 per cent of GDP in 1997, the major part of which was through private pension schemes. The share of private expenditure in gross total social expenditure in Denmark was 4.0 per cent, while in the United States it amounted to 35.7 per cent of GDP (Adema, 2001).

Total public spending, including other welfare state components, such as education and health, represented 54.3 per cent of GDP in 2000. Only in Sweden were government outlays higher (56.5 per cent). By comparison, the unweighted average for the four largest countries in Europe (France, Germany, Italy and the United Kingdom) was 44.1 per cent, while the rate for the United States was 32.0 per cent.

In recent years, in addition to gross social spending, the **net social expenditure** as a percentage of GDP has been used to measure effective social welfare levels. The net social expenditure rate takes into account the fact that, in countries like Denmark and the Netherlands, income from social transfers is subject to taxation just as any other income. Direct taxation and indirect taxes, such as value-added tax (which in Denmark is a significant source of financing for the welfare state), reduce the consumption power of social expenditure. In addition, the net social expenditure rate is adjusted for tax reductions or tax cuts, as for example negative income taxes for low-income earners in the United Kingdom and the United States (e.g. the earned income tax credit). Finally, in a variant of the net social expenditure rate used by Adema, two further components have been incorporated: private social outlays that are publicly mandated; and voluntary private social benefits that are publicly subsidized (Adema, 2001).

Denmark's net direct social expenditure rate falls substantially short of its gross rate of social spending. In 1997, the total net social expenditure for Denmark reached 27.5 per cent of GDP at factor cost (compared with 28.4 per cent in 1995), the third-highest rate in the OECD after Sweden (30.6 per cent) and Germany (28.8 per cent). The rate for United States was 23.4 per cent (figure 18). The lowest rate was recorded in Japan (15.7 per cent). The dispersion of net social expenditure rates is smaller than that of the gross rates. Gross public social expenditure in Denmark reached a level of 35.9 per cent of GDP at factor cost, and net public spending was 26.7 per cent of GDP. The difference of 9.2 percentage points is accounted for by direct taxes and social contributions (5.1 percentage points) and indirect taxes (4.1 percentage points) (Adema, 2001).

Voluntary and mandated social spending and public subsidies of private providence explain why, for the United States, the net total social spending rate exceeds the gross social expenditure by 8.3 percentage points. This has led commentators to speak of a "hidden private welfare state" in the United States. While the net social expenditure ratios in the OECD countries tend to converge, significant disparities remain in terms of public versus private social security schemes.

Expenditure on social protection in Denmark is largely financed from tax revenues, not from social contributions of employees and employers. In 1998, the proportion of social spending (supplementary benefits rather than social security contributions) financed by employers amounted to 8.7 per cent, by far the lowest in the EU-15. By comparison, the rate of employer financing of social spending

Figure 18   Social expenditure rates in the United States and Denmark, 1997

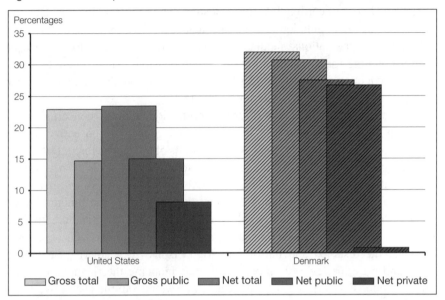

Source: Adema, 2001.

was 52.2 per cent in Spain, 50.6 per cent in Belgium, 46.5 per cent in France and 37.4 per cent in Germany (Eurostat and European Commission, 2001).

### Effects of social protection and welfare

Social welfare regimes have implications for effective social protection, income (re)distribution, poverty, the level and structure of employment, economic growth and social cohesion.

In Denmark, social transfer payments and social services are generally not, or only to a limited extent, dependent on previously earned income or labour market attachment. The level of compensation relative to previous income, in the case of unemployment, disability, maternity or sickness, is therefore higher for persons with low incomes. This is further reinforced through ceilings on benefits. Coupled with a progressive income tax scale, the social welfare system entails a considerable degree of income redistribution in favour of the lower income groups. Similar equalizing effects on income can be observed in the other Nordic countries. By contrast, in the United States, publicly sub-sidized private social pension, health, education and other welfare schemes tend to have regressive distributive effects and have therefore been favoured by the higher income groups; on the other hand, negative income taxes tend to have equalizing distributive effects at the lower end of the income spectrum.

Studies have estimated the poverty-reducing effect of social transfers in the European Union. According to a Eurostat study based on 1997 income data, the proportion of the population in Denmark that received an income of less than 60 per cent of the national median decreased from 30 per cent to 11 per cent after accounting for social transfers other than pensions. The average transfer-imputed reduction of poverty in 13 EU countries was from 26 per cent to 17 per cent (Eurostat and European Commission, 2001).

A further important effect of social protection regimes concerns social spending as an investment. In Denmark, many education and active labour market policies are geared to improving the skills of the labour force. Data from the EU countries indicate that the levels of literacy and of skills clearly covary with the degree of income equality. An active labour market policy provides a better match between supply and demand, thus improving the functioning of the labour market. A healthier labour force is more productive and creative. In so far as the public measures succeed in integrating groups such as elderly workers, the disabled and hard-to-employ persons, they enlarge the labour force and raise the level of employment, thus reducing the financial burdens on the State. Furthermore, to the extent that welfare diminishes poverty, it may help prevent crime, corruption and social disorder, and strengthen social cohesion. Shielding society from such negative effects may pay off in terms of a propitious business environment and climate for investment. In fact, as mentioned above, the Danish business community rates the Danish business environment very highly. Among all developed industrialized countries, Denmark is least affected by corruption, followed by Finland and Sweden. It enjoys one of the lowest crime rates in general and the lowest incidence of organized crime worldwide. Personal safety from physical attack is not only an element of the quality of life, but it represents a competitive advantage in attracting investment. The likelihood of being incarcerated in Denmark is low. The number of prisoners per 100,000 inhabitants was 67.4 in 1994. This compares with 95.0 in the United Kingdom, 117.9 in Canada and 553.9 in the United States (UNDP, 2001).

Social protection can facilitate trade and inward investment in another way. Workers who are well protected against income losses from structural adjustments tend to be less resistant to change, or positively speaking, are more willing to cooperate in product and process innovation. In fact, the countries with the most open economies have the highest level of social spending – among them, Denmark and the other Nordic countries, Austria, Germany and the Netherlands.

Some public social transfer payments, e.g. unemployment benefits, tend to rise during cyclical downturns in the economy, thus exerting a stabilizing effect on mass purchasing power through the business cycle, and in turn on aggregate demand in the labour market.

Trade union influence on the management and administration of the pension funds tends to have an impact on the profitability of enterprises. Employees who are not merely wage earners but also shareholders are inclined to take a long-term perspective on the development of their enterprise, and thus indirectly are concerned with employment security. Beyond that, it has been an objective of the investment policy of the labour market pension system to support structural change in the economy, and avoid maintaining uncompetitive sectors. In recent years, ethical standards for investment by the pension funds have been formulated. These include not making investments in violation of international agreements and conventions (Buck, 2000).

The relationship between social protection regimes and employment is complex, and not easy to assess. Unemployment benefits provide not only income support for unemployed workers, but also the economic means for workers to search for suitable employment in line with their skills, rather than having to take the first job available. However, benefits are conditional on effective job search and on participation in active labour market programmes. It is widely held, notably by the economic orthodoxy, that high personal income taxes and high tax wedges, i.e. the proportion of earnings taken in income taxes and social security contributions by employers and employees, reduce the financial returns from work, thereby discouraging the supply of labour. Tax introduces a wedge between the employer's labour cost and the employee's take-home pay. Social security contributions from employers would lower the demand for labour, by reducing profitability and investment, and encouraging the substitution of labour by capital. It has also been argued that countries with egalitarian wage and income distributions are less capable of creating employment in the low-wage sectors, thereby constraining employment generation in the aggregate.

Denmark has comparatively low rates of social contributions. The proportion of non-wage costs in total labour costs was 6.3 per cent in 1999, compared with 20.7 per cent in the United States, 28.1 per cent in Sweden, and 31.8 per cent in France (ILO, 2002). However, Denmark has very high income and consumption tax rates and very low income inequality. At the same time, Denmark has the highest employment rate, and the lowest rate of structural unemployment, in the EU. So, taking everything together, the Danish case provides weak support for the orthodox position. Labour market activity in Denmark and other Nordic countries has obviously been encouraged rather than discouraged by public provisions such as maternity and parental leave schemes, and care for children and the elderly, because they have allowed women to work. But Denmark may also support the case for tax-financed, rather than contribution-financed, social protection. Alternatively, if social protection is not financed through taxes it must be financed from private sources. This is clearly demonstrated by the case of the United States, where a high rate of private spending raises considerably the level of total social expenditure.

Employment in Denmark seems to have benefited from the high level of personal and social services. In the EU-15 countries, the aggregate employment rate is strongly linked to the proportion of employment in social and personal services. Higher employment rates for women have led to additional sources of funding for social security. Moreover, studies have concluded that employment in the private sector has not been sensitive to a high level of taxation and social charges. In economic sectors exposed to international competition, high-tax countries like Austria, Denmark, Germany, and Sweden have attained higher employment rates than the United States with its much lower taxation level (Scharpf, 2000).

The acceptance of taxation by the citizens does not appear to depend on the level of taxes. Quite the contrary, where income and consumption taxes are high, but are efficiently spent and redistributed, tax revolts and tax evasion seem to be less frequent. The perceived returns on taxation, in the form of wider opportunities, equity and insurance for all, may be the more important factors for tax morale.

Finally, the best form of social security is decent work, i.e. jobs that pay a living wage and are not constantly at risk. In this sense, Denmark may be said to exhibit high social security, in addition to its high security for those who cannot work. Informalization does not play the big role in Denmark (and the other Nordic countries) that it does in many other countries worldwide. Denmark's employment is overwhelmingly formal. Informal employment is not even measured, and is certainly not a prime topic of debate. At least in part, this may be attributed to the public revenue financing of social protection, instead of payroll tax financing which may lead workers and employers to seek non-formal work.

## Gender equality

The Danish welfare state, based on principles of universalism, egalitarianism and social inclusion, aims to promote equality not only with regard to income distribution but also between women and men.

The following elements tend to support gender equality (Tiainen, 1999):

- The "dual-earner" model: employment of men *and* women is seen as the normal and desirable means for securing income and supporting oneself and one's children, and for attaining independence and autonomy in shaping one's individual life pattern.

- A system of individual rights supports entry and stay in the labour market.
- Public services allow high participation of women in the labour force, in particular for women with small children.
- Earnings-related compensation in periods of joblessness maintains the individual's contact with the labour market.
- Individual taxation, together with a high marginal tax rate and small wage differentials, serves as an incentive to having two wage earners in the household. Both income earners can also contribute to their own pension, based on their respective earnings.
- There are various provisions (fiscal incentives as well as services) to reconcile work and family needs, such as childcare facilities, parental leave and care for the elderly.
- Access for all to high-quality free education is a major dimension of gender equality.

The Danish welfare model can be distinguished from other welfare regimes in its approach to gender equality (Esping-Andersen, 1990; Palme, 1999). According to the *"male-breadwinner" model*, childcare and other functions are seen as the responsibilities of women who do not seek employment or full employment. In this model, rights and economic incentives that promote gender equality are less developed. Social security entitlements of non-working women are derived rights, based on the insurance of the male breadwinner. There may also be differences in the rates of benefits or contributions between men and women.

The male-breadwinner model dominated in the industrialized countries for most of the twentieth century. It began to be eroded first in the Nordic countries, then in North America. It is still fairly prevalent in continental European countries, where the "home-caring society" is still deeply anchored. It may shrink further as countries implement the European Union goal of employment rates of 60 per cent for women, and 70 per cent for women and men together, by the year 2010.

Under the *"Anglo-Saxon" model*, both men and women would seek employment to earn a living, but public social security provisions and social services are less developed, thus reducing the choice between activity and non-activity in the labour market. Care facilities that are organized on a private basis cannot be afforded equally by every household, leading to greater inequalities than in the Nordic model.

While gender and family structures have recently changed in Europe and other OECD countries, the gender work patterns described above are still clearly visible. The proportion of dual earners in the Nordic countries is substantially higher than elsewhere – 92 per cent of all households in Sweden and 89 per cent in Finland are dual-earning (Anxo et al., 1999). Consequently, the proportion of single male earners is much lower than in other OECD countries. The male breadwinner model is still an important feature in Germany (31 per cent), Netherlands (47 per cent) and Belgium (36 per cent), but not in Denmark, Sweden and Finland. The "Anglo-Saxon" countries assume an intermediate position between the Nordic and the continental EU countries.

A number of policies paved the way for the transformation from the male-breadwinner system to the dual-earner system. These included improved access of women to higher education and vocational skills training; leave arrangements for employed parents; making the environment and organization of the workplace responsive to the needs of workers with children; the expansion of public childcare and care for the elderly; and adjustments in the system of taxation to provide incentives for married women to enter paid employment. The proportion of children under 3 years of age using formal (public or private) childcare arrangements is highest in Denmark (64 per cent compared with an average of 26.2 per cent for the OECD-20). On a composite OECD index measuring work/family reconciliation policies and related flexible work arrangements, Denmark scores highest among 18 OECD countries. The employment rate of 78.8 per cent for women aged 30–34 years is also the highest (OECD average 67.2 per cent), and is largely explained by public policy measures that enable young parents to work and meet their family and child-rearing responsibilities (OECD, 2001a). The avoidance of low pay, excessive working hours, and holding of multiple jobs ("moonlighting") is also conducive to reconciling family life and work.

Welfare state arrangements have played a central role in the dramatic increase of employment for women, particularly the expansion of public social services and health care. In 1999, 51.4 per cent of Danish women were employed in the public sector compared with 25.1 per cent of Danish men (Statistics Denmark, 2000). By 1997, the proportion of female employees in health and social work had reached 83.4 per cent, the third-highest level in Europe after Finland (89.9 per cent) and Sweden (86.3 per cent) (European Foundation, 2001). There is comparatively high horizontal sex segregation, based on occupation and sector, in the Danish labour market. According to an index of dissimilarity, the Nordic countries (here Finland, Norway and Sweden) lead the industrialized world in the manifestation of "male" and "female" occupations, even after segregation levels had declined in the 1970s and 1980s (Melkas and Anker, 1998). This is in part a reflection of the high labour force participation of women. A recent study in Denmark reached similar conclusions, suggesting that in total private sector employment, nearly 4 workers in 10 would have to change occupation and function to achieve an equal distribution between women and men (DA, 2001). However, it should be noted that occupational segregation by sex does not necessarily imply discrimination in access to jobs or at the workplace. General social and cultural determinants may shape occupational segregation far more than discrimination. Vertical sex segregation (the relative concentration of women in low-status positions) continues to exist, but is decreasing.

One simple indicator of occupational segregation by sex is relative wage levels. At the end of the 1990s, the average hourly wage of women in Denmark was 80 per cent of that of men. Some 22 per cent (or 4.5 percentage points) of the gap can be attributed to differences within the workplace (working hours, educational attainment, work experience, seniority), while another 43 per cent (8.5 percentage points) relates to the fact that women are employed in different sectors from men (public services rather than trade and manufacturing in the private sector), with the remaining 35 per cent (7 percentage points) unaccounted for (LO, 2001). A similar study suggested that differences in average wages ranged from 15.4 per cent in the private sector to 25.7 per cent in the public sector, with only 3 to 4 percentage points unaccounted for (DA, 2001). As part of the mainstreaming principle of public policy, the Ministry of Labour is drawing up a strategy for reducing occupational sex segregation in the Danish labour market, based on experience in three pilot regions. The guiding principle is the elimination of all obstacles to the free and informed choice of occupation for both women and men.

## Labour market and training policies

Institutional and policy learning seems to have brought about a real turnaround in the Danish labour market in recent years. The market is in many ways idiosyncratic, in particular in its interactions with the labour market institutions and policies. These institutions (such as active labour market policies, labour market training authorities and the public employment service) are strongly influenced by the social partners at the national, regional and local levels.

The labour market institutions were not created by design in one stroke. Rather, they are the outcome of policy learning in the course of collective bargaining processes. As a result, a mix has been found between policies for welfare and equity, on the one hand, and efficiency and competition, on the other. The government is an active player in this bargaining, not only because of the importance of public services and its role as an employer, but also as a provider of institutional support to both business and labour, facilitating their participation and social dialogue (Auer, 2000).

The Danish labour market is an integral part of the socioeconomic system and the welfare state. More than in other countries, the welfare state is built on the participation in employment of both women and men, as reflected in the high employment-to-population ratios for both sexes. The next section, "Interaction between microeconomic and macroeconomic policy", will present the specific macroeconomic conditions of the welfare state, such as the structurally large share of government expenditure in GDP, which does not prevent a commitment to stability-oriented growth with low inflation, moderate wage increases, low interest rates and a stable currency exchange rate in relation to its main European trading partners (supported by Denmark's entry into the ERM-2 currency band for non EMU members).

## The golden triangle of "flexicurity"

Contemporary labour market policy in Denmark has been described as a "golden triangle" (figure 19). The corners of this triangle consist of:

– a flexible labour market characterized by comparatively weak employment protection legislation (partly supplemented by collective bargaining agreements for certain sectors, especially with regard to dismissal notice periods);
– generous income protection in case of unemployment;
– an encompassing active labour market policy, including extensive training programmes enabling the unemployed to return to work as soon as possible ("learnfare").

In the OECD index of the strictness of employment protection, which covers different components of labour legislation, such as statutory notice periods, dismissal procedures, severance pay and rules governing unfair dismissal, Denmark ranks (by order of increasing protection strictness) at number 8 of 26 countries. But Denmark is first (among 27 OECD countries) for spending on labour market policies (OECD, 2001a), and for the growth of that spending. Denmark has one of the highest levels of unemployment benefits and relatively long passive and active benefit periods.

This combination of regulatory elements makes it relatively easy for firms to dismiss workers (and easy for workers to quit firms), while laid-off workers are fairly well protected against loss of both income and employability. Access to publicly financed training is easy and everybody has access to the public employment service. Active labour market policies, dominated by training measures, also include direct job creation and employment subsidies, as well as measures for the disabled. Within the toolbox of labour market policies are also parental leave schemes (the former sabbatical and educational leave schemes have now been abandoned). A specific instrument is the job rotation scheme, through which unemployed people replace those in temporary training or on parental leave. Despite the emphasis on active policies (among EU countries, Denmark is the

Figure 19   The golden triangle of "flexicurity"

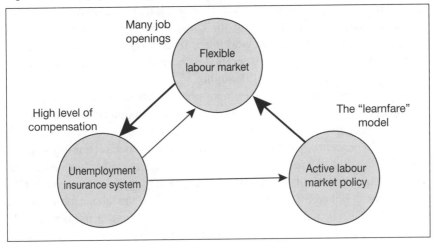

Source: Madsen, 2001.

second-highest spender on active policies after the Netherlands), temporary "passive" income replacement, through the unemployment benefit scheme and permanent withdrawal from the labour market through early retirement schemes, is still more important in relative spending terms (expenditures on active and passive measures stand in a relation of about 1 to 3). It is recalled that unemployment benefits are conditional upon availability and willingness to work.

The interaction between private and public labour markets and labour market institutions in the setting of the golden triangle gives a unique model of labour market functioning and accounts for both the high labour mobility and the high security among the workforce. If anywhere, it is in Denmark where a system of "flexicurity" has been institutionalized for a significant proportion of the workforce. It is this arrangement that allows for employment adjustment, labour mobility and employability.

### Institutionally mediated mobility

The golden triangle seems to underpin Denmark's high mobility rates. Depending on the data and methods used, Denmark comes third (retrospective labour force survey data) or fourth (European household panel data) among the countries of the EU (mobility being measured as the sum of flows into and out of salaried employment). Madsen (2001) showed that annual labour turnover was around 30 per cent of the labour force. High mobility is also reflected in considerable flows between employment and unemployment, where Denmark ranks third in Europe (after Greece and Spain) (Kruppe, 2001). In Denmark mobility is more equally distributed among the workforce than, for example, in Spain. There, the high mobility largely reflects the number of young people on temporary contracts, and the labour market is strongly segmented between a stable and a flexible part of the workforce. In contrast, Denmark has a much lower proportion of temporary workers, less segmented labour markets, and a lower degree of concentration of flexibility.

The main difference from other high-mobility labour markets, such as the United States, is the proportion of workers transiting through labour market institutions. Two figures illustrate this: between 1997 and 2000, each year an average of around 19 per cent of the labour force entered a labour market training scheme, while 22 per cent had a period of unemployment. Taken together (not accounting for recurrences), this adds up to around 41 per cent of the labour force (OECD, 2001a). In the United States only about 0.7 per cent of the labour force enters a public training scheme every year, and around 15 per cent of the labour force experiences a period of unemployment (data estimated on the basis of 1985 flows). As average duration of unemployment in Denmark is one of the shortest in Europe and, furthermore, training courses are comparatively short, these large flows correspond to quite small proportions of the labour force who are unemployed (4.7 per cent in 2000) or in training (around 2.9 per cent in 1999) at any given time. Whereas in the United States mobility is "market-driven" and few mediating institutions exist, labour mobility in Denmark, while still market-driven, is mediated through labour market institutions. These different systems both result in high labour mobility but the consequences in terms of security of income and employability are very different. While job loss in the United States is associated with considerable income loss, Danish workers (especially those with below-average earnings) are fairly well protected and have opportunities to enter training and other labour market programmes. It has been shown that high replacement levels in the Danish income compensation schemes contribute to a more egalitarian income distribution and thus greater social cohesion.

There is another outstanding feature: it is often claimed that a generous income-replacement scheme for unemployed workers produces disincentives to work. However, the Danish case does not exemplify this: the employment rate is one of the highest in the world, unemployment spells are shorter than elsewhere in Europe, the long-term unemployment rate has come down to 1 per cent (ILO, 2002) and the number of "marginalized" workers, i.e. those who have difficulties finding market jobs, fell from 127,000 in 1994 to 60,000 in 1998 and approximately 50,000 in 2000 (Ministry of Labour, key data). The same can be said about the labour market training system: it is designed to accommodate short-term training needs of companies and workers, as well as the longer-term training needs of the unemployed. It seems also to be highly adaptable to the prevailing labour market situation: in 2000 about two-thirds of people entering labour market training were employed adults, while in years of high unemployment the unemployed usually dominate. This change in inflows could also be linked to the recently (January 2001) enacted reform of the labour market vocational training system, and the reform (January 2000) of the financing of training programmes for unemployed.

Proactive measures that allow workers to become eligible for training before they become unemployed, together with a policy of "activation of the unemployed", may explain why Denmark has the lowest rate of "structural unemployment" in the EU-15, according to some estimates (Lönnroth, 2000). Structural unemployment comprises those who are long-term unemployed and those who are inactive but nevertheless looking for a job. In 1998, this rate was 26.9 per cent in Denmark, but 51.5 per cent in Germany, 61.7 per cent in Belgium, and 67.3 per cent in Italy. For the EU-15, the (unweighted) average rate was 49.4 per cent. The other Nordic countries also had low structural unemployment: Finland had a rate of 27.5 per cent and Sweden 37.4 per cent.

Denmark exhibits by far the lowest rate of "potential structural unemployment", as measured by the yearly average inflow into long-term unemployment. This amounted to 3.3 per cent in 1998, compared with 5.0 per cent in Sweden, 5.4 per cent in Austria, and 11.3 per cent in Finland. The average rate for the EU-15 stood at 11.4 per cent. The "potential effective labour supply", measured as total unemployment less the sum of structural unemployment and the inflow into long-term unemployment, as a percentage of all unemployed, reached 69.8 per cent in Denmark, the highest for this indicator, and far above the average value for the EU-15 of 39.2 per cent (Lönnroth, 2000). The implication is that the higher the effective labour supply, the more compatible it is with low and stable inflation, and therefore with flexible monetary policy in support of an employment-friendly macroeconomic policy.

As can be seen in figure 20, Denmark's unemployment rate is much more volatile than the EU average. This shows a strong elasticity of unemployment with economic growth. The United States has a similar pattern, albeit with lower unemployment peaks since the mid-seventies. However, unlike the other EU countries, Denmark seems not to be affected by a ratchet effect: in the EU (reflecting basically the situation in the larger EU countries), unemployment levels were higher at each new onset of a recession (3 per cent in 1973–74), 6 per cent in the early 1980s and 8 per cent in the early 1990s, posing a big challenge to policy makers. In Denmark (and the United States) this was true only for the second oil shock in the early 1980s (6 per cent unemployment compared with virtually none in 1973–74). Unlike many EU countries, unemployment was below 6 per cent at the onset of the recession of the 1990s,

Figure 20   Unemployment rate as percentage of total labour force, 1970–2000

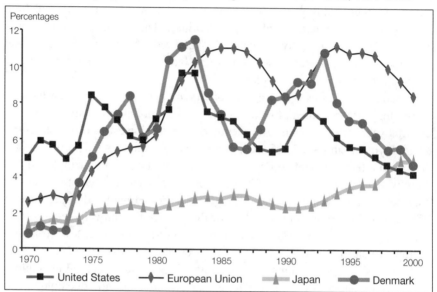

Source: OECD, 2001a.

and is now – probably at the onset of a new period of sluggish world growth – clearly even lower. Such a development, in a labour market where the unemployed are well protected by income replacement, training and other active labour market policies, shows that both flexibility and security can work. (For a similar cyclical pattern of unemployment, coverage levels for both income replacement and active labour market policies are much higher in Denmark than in the United States).

Of course, labour market policies in Denmark are not without costs. In the second half of the 1990s, Denmark spent more than any other OECD country on labour market measures. In 2000, the total public expenditure on such measures was about 4.5 per cent of GDP. By comparison, the Netherlands spent 3.7 per cent, Finland 3.3 per cent, Sweden 2.7 per cent, Japan 0.8 per cent and the United States less than 0.4 per cent. Denmark spent over 1.5 per cent of GDP on active labour market measures, at a par with the Netherlands and ahead of Sweden. In 1997, when unemployment was higher, spending in Denmark was 5.5 per cent of GDP, while the average rate for the EU-15 was 1.1 per cent, and for the OECD 0.8 per cent (OECD, 2001a). In 2000, the inflow of participants into active labour market measures in Denmark was 21.0 per cent of the labour force, a rate that no other country came anywhere near (in 1997, the EU-15 average was 10.3 per cent, the OECD rate 8.1 per cent, while Denmark reached around 24 per cent) (table 7).

Table 7 Labour market policy expenditure and participant inflows in Denmark, 1997–2000

| Programme categories | Public expenditure as a percentage of GDP | | | | Participant inflows as a percentage of the labour force | | | |
|---|---|---|---|---|---|---|---|---|
| | 1997 | 1998 | 1999 | 2000 | 1997 | 1998 | 1999 | 2000 |
| **1. Public employment services and administration** | **0.12** | **0.12** | **0.11** | **0.11** | **n.a** | **n.a** | **n.a** | **n.a** |
| **2. Labour market training** | **0.93** | **0.96** | **0.97** | **0.84** | **18.47** | **20.62** | **19.72** | **15.78** |
| a) of unemployed adults and those at risk | 0.64 | 0.71 | 0.77 | 0.66 | 8.82 | 12.46 | 11.64 | 5.71 |
| b) of employed adults | 0.28 | 0.25 | 0.21 | 0.18 | 9.65 | 8.16 | 8.09 | 10.07 |
| **3. Measures for unemployed and disadvantaged young people** | **0.10** | **0.08** | **0.12** | **0.10** | **1.50** | **1.50** | **1.88** | **1.82** |
| **4. Subsidized employment** | **0.30** | **0.27** | **0.23** | **0.17** | **1.11** | **1.05** | **1.00** | **0.81** |
| a) subsidies to regular employment in the private sector | 0.02 | 0.02 | 0.02 | 0.02 | 0.22 | 0.25 | 0.22 | 0.20 |
| b) support of unemployed persons starting enterprises | 0.06 | 0.04 | 0.01 | – | 0.10 | – | – | – |
| c) direct job creation (public or non-profit) | 0.22 | 0.21 | 0.19 | 0.15 | 0.78 | 0.78 | 0.78 | 0.62 |
| **5. Measures for the disabled – vocational rehabilitation** | **0.21** | **0.24** | **0.32** | **0.33** | **2.28** | **2.51** | **3.05** | **2.56** |
| **6. Unemployment compensation** | **2.12** | **1.67** | **1.41** | **1.33** | **24.42** | **23.08** | **21.15** | **19.46** |
| **7. Early retirement for labour market reasons** | **1.71** | **1.70** | **1.68** | **1.63** | **1.06** | **1.06** | **0.58** | **0.97** |
| **TOTAL** | **5.49** | **5.04** | **4.84** | **4.51** | **48.84** | **49.82** | **47.38** | **41.40** |
| Active measures (1–5) | 1.66 | 1.66 | 1.76 | 1.54 | 23.37 | 25.69 | 25.66 | 20.97 |
| Passive measures (6 and 7) | 3.83 | 3.37 | 3.09 | 2.96 | 25.48 | 24.15 | 21.72 | 20.44 |
| *For reference* | | | | | | | | |
| GDP (national currency, at current prices, billions) | 1 116 | 1 169 | 1 230 | 1 312 | | | | |
| Labour force (thousands) | | | | | 2 856 | 2 848 | 2 865 | 2 875 |

n.a. = not applicable;  – = data not available

Source:  OECD, 2001a.

## Initial vocational training and education

The effectiveness of adult labour market training, and of active labour market policies as a whole, hinges a good deal on the basic vocational training of young people. The better the basic skills of the labour force, the easier it will normally be for them to acquire additional skills, update their skills, or undergo retraining for other occupations.

Denmark has established an effective basic vocational and technical training system. It combines initial basic training and further training, the latter being organized as short and long modules. After completing the nine years of *Folkeskole* (primary and lower secondary school), 96 per cent of young people aged 17-19 are enrolled in youth education, and almost 60 per cent of these enter vocational education and training (VET) programmes, which normally last three years. The remainder undertake upper secondary education or adult education. The basic vocational education and training is based on the 2000 Act on Vocational Education and Training, which replaced the 1956 Apprenticeship Act and the 1977 Act on Basic Vocational Education. VET is organized around the principle of "dual" education, combining theoretical instruction in vocational schools with practical training in an enterprise. For each of the 87 occupation-oriented courses (compared with 300 in the past), a trade committee representing employer organizations and trade unions plays a central role in determining the professional content and the curriculum, and setting standards for the apprentices' final examinations (OECD, 1998c; CEDEFOP, 1994).

High-quality comprehensive vocational training is regarded as a national goal in Denmark, for which business, labour and the Government share responsibility. There is a consensus that all young people should have a basic vocational qualification. Enterprises are closely involved in vocational training, which is directly related to work and carried out close to the workplace. Tripartite social dialogue plays a critical role in the design and implementation of vocational training policies.

Despite this favourable training environment, critics of the system have pointed out that it is often difficult for young people to find the practical internships they need for their vocational training, and that there is a gap between the training given in the vocational schools and the skills needed in companies. Such criticism has also been extended to the adult training and has led to the recent reform of the employment service. This service has now been charged with two somewhat contradictory aims: to target the training needs of companies, and to focus more on the needs of those groups most difficult to place in the labour market.

## Too good to be true?

According to Madsen (2001), the benefits of the "golden triangle" are widely accepted and no major reform effort seems to be necessary. The system seems to be functional for a highly developed welfare state and to strike a balance between efficiency and equity. It allows for competitive adjustment of employment and progress in employability, and provides income security. The feeling of job insecurity is comparatively low in Denmark. In 2000, 49 per cent of French employees, 54 per cent in the United States, and 65 per cent of Japanese were worried about the future of their company, compared with only 43 per cent of the Danish workers surveyed. Furthermore, 37 per cent of the French and the Americans, 38 per cent of the Japanese, and only 20 per cent of the Danes were unsure of the security of the job they held, even if they performed well. The Danish rate was the lowest in the EU, and had even improved since 1996, when 32 per cent had had doubts about their job security (OECD, 2001a).

The Danish labour market has not always performed as well as it does at present. As recently as 1993, Denmark had unemployment levels of over 10 per cent. But by a combination of renewed economic growth – stimulated by a short-term fiscal boost through a tax cut – and labour market reforms initiated by the Government and designed in cooperation with the social partners, the situation improved dramatically. The labour market reform of 1993, and its subsequent amendments, were based on the concepts of "activation" and "employability" and changed both active and passive labour market policy. Every insured unemployed worker (over 80 per cent of the unemployed are insured) nowadays has a "right" to activation, i.e. to be offered a job or a training slot after no more than 12 months of joblessness (within six months for workers under 25 years of age), but also has an obligation to accept the offer in order to continue to be entitled to public financial support.

While income replacement rates for unemployed workers remained unaltered, the duration of eligibility for benefit was severely cut, in several steps. Today, the total period of receipt of benefit is four years, down from eight years before the reform. As noted above, activation of insured unemployed workers must start before the end of the first year of "passive" receipt of benefit for adults and before six months for young people. However, because of simultaneous individual counselling and accompaniment, job search and matching are actually intensified before activation starts. It was also ruled that participation in labour market schemes no longer leads to requalifying for benefit. In addition, the work availability rule and eligibility criteria have been tightened (Callesen, 2000a). In 1998, a law was passed to activate employment policy at the level of municipalities, and in 1999, legal provisions were adopted to increase the opportunities for the employment of foreigners and the integration of immigrants and refugees (many of whom are not in the labour market). These measures were taken at a point when supply shortages in the Danish labour market had become more apparent. The tightening of the labour market has also benefited foreigners, leading to a fall in their unemployment rates. Denmark has clearly pursued the goal of integrating more people into the labour market. It has progressed towards a more active welfare state, with rights to social transfers contingent on the individual's participation in paid activities, rather than on long periods of passive replacement of income.

The active labour market in Denmark is not totally new. Active measures to fight mass unemployment, including training and public job creation, were taken during the economic depression in the 1930s (Greve, 2000). Special programmes to build roads and bridges served to improve public infrastructure. The general idea behind an active labour market policy is that public intervention is needed to remedy market failures leading to involuntary unemployment. In contrast to earlier periods, activation during the past decade has been primarily geared to extending and upgrading labour market skills, with a view to maintaining Denmark's position in international competition.

Although the improvement in the labour market, especially concerning long-term unemployment, might give credit to the success of supply-side-oriented labour market reforms, this is only part of the story. The reform coincided with, and benefited from, an economic upswing triggered by a number of other factors, including a fine-tuned expansionary macroeconomic policy in the early 1990s. This raised aggregate demand for labour in conditions of macroeconomic stability. In the absence of this higher economic growth, the activation strategy would probably have been much less successful.

The Danish case lends support to the view that the causes of unemployment are found on both the supply and the demand sides of the labour market. It shows that policies play an important role in coping with employment problems. However, passive as well as active measures have contributed to the Danish success. The recent focus on active policies is an important policy change, but it has limits in a country in which short periods of unemployment are frequent and constitute an adjustment buffer for companies. Labour market policies require high tax rates for their financing. But both firms and workers benefit from them because they allow wage costs to be "socialized" – especially important for small firms – improve employability, and allow a better match between supply and demand in the labour market.

In summary, Denmark has achieved a well-functioning labour market, incorporating both flexibility and workers' security. As Madsen notes: "… the lack of reform plans in the Danish agenda of labour market policy does at least indicate that the main political actors seem to share the view that the present balance in the trade-off between flexibility and social protection is not too far from the optimum" (Madsen, 2001, p.58).

Table 8    Decomposition of GDP per capita, 1998 US$ at PPP

| | GDP per hour (PPP $) | Average annual hours worked per employed person | Employment to working-age population ratio | Adjustment coefficient for employment in 16–64 age group[a] | Working-age population as a percentage of total population | GDP per capita (PPP $) |
|---|---|---|---|---|---|---|
| Austria | 37.75 | 1 515 | 61.0 | 1.0087 | 68.0 | 23 930 |
| Belgium | 39.27 | 1 635 | 57.0 | 1.0074 | 65.7 | 24 239 |
| Canada | 30.37 | 1 768 | 68.9 | 1.0037 | 68.7 | 25 496 |
| Denmark | 33.67 | 1 527 | 75.3 | 1.0110 | 66.9 | 26 176 |
| France | 35.47 | 1 599 | 59.4 | 1.0116 | 65.3 | 22 255 |
| Germany | 34.93 | 1 580 | 59.0 | 1.0314 | 68.1 | 22 856 |
| Italy | 37.46 | 1 648 | 51.8 | 1.0227 | 68.0 | 22 234 |
| Japan | 25.64 | 1 842 | 69.5 | 1.0712 | 68.7 | 24 170 |
| Netherlands | 37.33 | 1 368 | 69.4 | 1.0027 | 67.6 | 24 008 |
| Norway | 38.55 | 1 401 | 78.3 | 1.0132 | 64.4 | 27 581 |
| Sweden | 29.74 | 1 551 | 71.5 | 1.0254 | 62.7 | 21 218 |
| United Kingdom | 29.44 | 1 587 | 71.2 | 1.0069 | 64.2 | 21 502 |
| United States | 35.95 | 1 833 | 73.8 | 1.0168 | 65.6 | 32 413 |

[a] The adjustment coefficient corrects the employment rate for employed persons not included in the 16–64 age group who nevertheless contribute to GDP.

Sources: Bureau of Labor Statistics, 2000b; OECD, 2001a (employment rates); Scarpetta et al., 2000 (working time).

The Danish experience shows that decent work is not delivered by individual enterprises or the public sector alone. Security of employment, employability and income stretches beyond the frontier of the individual firm. It is through the interplay of enterprises and labour market institutions that decent work can flourish and be maintained through the peaks and troughs of economic activity.

## Interaction between microeconomic and macroeconomic policy

Denmark provides an interesting illustration of the strong linkages between the labour market, social welfare and overall economic growth. Underlying these linkages are integrated micro- and macroeconomic policies. Consider the following: Denmark has achieved a very high level of GDP per capita (US$26,176 in 1998 at PPP, or 80 per cent of the level in the United States (table 8). This is a result of high labour productivity (GDP per hour at 93.7 per cent of the United States level), annual working hours close to the European

Table 9     Employment to working-age population ratios (15–64 years), 2000

|  | Men (25–54 years) | Women (25–54 years) | Aged workers (55–64 years) | Young workers (15–24 years) | Total |
|---|---|---|---|---|---|
| Denmark | 88.3 | 80.4 | 54.6 | 67.1 | 76.4 |
| France | 87.0 | 69.6 | 34.2 | 23.3 | 61.1 |
| Germany | 89.4 | 70.8 | 38.6 | 48.4 | 66.3 |
| Netherlands | 92.2 | 70.9 | 37.9 | 68.4 | 72.9 |
| Spain | 85.4 | 50.7 | 36.8 | 35.9[a] | 56.1 |
| Sweden | 85.8 | 81.7 | 65.1 | 46.1[a] | 74.2 |
| United Kingdom | 87.5 | 73.1 | 50.5 | 61.5[a] | 72.4 |
| United States | 89.0 | 74.3 | 57.7 | 59.8[a] | 74.1 |

[a] 16–24 year age group.

Source: OECD, 2001a.

average (83.3 per cent of the United States level) and a very high employment-to-population ratio (102 per cent of the ratio in the United States). Denmark is thus both a highly efficient and a labour-intensive economy, through which it enjoys high living standards. This can be seen as a combination of efficient labour market policies, a high level of social protection, sound macroeconomic policies and strong institutions.

On the side of the labour market, there are at least three factors that account for the high income level achieved in Denmark. First, there is a high level of labour input. The most striking element here is the very high proportion of the population of working age who are employed, second-highest in the OECD after Norway. This proportion is particularly high among the young, suggesting that the transition from education and training to employment is a particularly successful one in Denmark. Alternatively, it implies that young people are either in education or in employment or both, and that few are neither studying nor employed. The range of policies aimed at adapting the educational and training system to the changing skills requirements of the labour force attests to a relatively smooth transition from school to work. The youth unemployment rate in 2000 was 1.4 times higher than the aggregate unemployment rate, compared with 1.9 in the EU-15. The employment rate is equally high among adult women. This reflects a genuine commitment to gender equality, as reflected in an array of public services and entitlements that help young parents with children reconcile their family responsibilities with their work. The much higher proportion of women working in the public sector than in the private sector underlines a certain level of occupational segregation, which may point to more fundamental and as yet unresolved gender inequities.

The employment rate among aged workers (55–64 years) is high in Denmark, but lower than in Sweden and the United States (table 9). This reflects the policy option of early retirement (or labour shedding as termed by Esping-Andersen, 1996) which emerged during the period of high unemployment up to 1995–96 and which was revised by the social partners and the Government in 1999 in order to provide economic incentives in an effort to discourage early retirement.

The consequence of these comparatively high employment ratios is that most households have at least two income earners (although 20 per cent of all households in Denmark have only one adult member against 16 per cent for the EU-15) and that a significant proportion of people of working age both contribute to the production of goods and services and benefit from the public services and entitlements financed through income taxation. The redistribution operating through taxation and public services allows a high degree of labour force participation, particularly of women, and ensures a relatively high level of labour productivity.

The other element to be considered under labour input is the number of working hours. With 1,527 hours worked on average in 1999, Denmark is below the European average of approximately 1,600 hours, and much lower than either Japan or the United States. This reflects a collective preference for shorter working hours, with a relatively short working week (37 hours) and a standard five weeks holiday per year, rather than a preference for part-time work. Annual working time has been relatively stable in Denmark since 1984, with a slight decline up to 1991 and an increase since.

The second factor in the labour market is the level of labour productivity – output per hour worked or per employed person. At US$33.67 (PPP) per hour worked in 1998, Denmark is close to the average for the high labour productivity countries, lower than Austria, Belgium, France, Germany and the United States, but higher than Canada, Japan and Sweden. This is a reflection of the excellent health, education and social protection services found in Denmark, as well as the high standard of working conditions in enterprises and high levels of worker participation. The Republic of Korea apart, the average annual growth in labour productivity in Denmark, at 3.2 per cent over the 1990s, was the highest of the OECD countries. It also illustrates the composition of output, with manufacturing accounting for a relatively small share of both value added and employment (approximately 17.0 per cent in 1999), a high proportion of small firms, and a high level of public and personal services (35 per cent of employment and 28 per cent of gross value added). The cost of high-quality education and health services, and social protection for all, is most likely recovered in lower spending on police, prison and social aid, and a much higher quality of life, which is also reflected in high labour productivity. There are very few low-productivity, low-wage jobs in Denmark, in spite of a large public service sector.

The third factor in the labour market is labour costs. A high employment ratio, a high proportion of wage earners in total employment (92.0 per cent), and a high proportion of wages in total value added (total employee compensation represented 63.1 per cent of gross domestic income in 1999) imply a high sensitivity of domestic demand, production costs and enterprise competitiveness to adjustments in labour costs. As the share of non-wage labour costs is unusually low in Denmark, the significant variable here is the total wage bill. By accepting real wage increases compatible with stable inflation, the social partners have implicitly adopted a policy of wage restraint. Unit labour costs in fact increased at a more moderate pace over the 1990s than in other countries, although the rate tended to accelerate in the second half, reflecting both higher growth in output and lower unemployment. The capacity of the social partners to maintain the implicit wage restraint policy in the face of inevitably mounting shortages of labour supply in the short term (lower unemployment) and the longer term (ageing of the population) represents perhaps the single most important challenge facing the Danish people.

Comparing Denmark with other high-income countries, the particular combination of productive inputs puts the emphasis on labour input (high employment rate), with average hourly productivity and working time on the low side. This can be compared with the United States, for instance, which stresses all three elements, or with other countries that emphasize only one (high hourly productivity in Austria or Italy, but with low employment rates in both cases) or two (high employment rates and hourly productivity, as in Norway). The critical questions behind these different combinations are whether the particular institutional settings can sustain them, and whether the distributions behind the aggregate averages fully reflect freedom of choice.

Real GDP growth in Denmark averaged 2.1 per cent during the period 1989–99 (OECD, 2000a). However the rate was much higher between 1994 and 1999 than between 1989 and 1994 (3.0 per cent and 0.6 per cent respectively). The difference is attributable essentially to domestic macroeconomic policy, although the supportive external environment played an important role as well. Since the early 1990s distinct macroeconomic policy choices have been made which closely paralleled labour market policy choices. Fiscal balance became a priority, following the brief expansionary stimulus of 1993, which boosted internal demand but was quickly balanced by higher external demand. Labour market policy aimed at increasing flexibility, and putting more people back into employment by improving their skills, thereby reducing the number of persons on unemployment benefits, but not reducing the level of these benefits.

Balancing of the budget was thus achieved, not by slashing expenditures, but rather through reduced spending on unemployment, as macroeconomic policy steered the economy towards a higher growth path, in which both domestic demand and exports were significant. This illustrates how closely the important macroeconomic objective of fiscal balance is linked to developments in the labour market. At the same time, lower inflation became an explicit objective and was facilitated by the implicit wage restraint policy, which itself was dependent on reduced inflationary expectations, in part a product of a lower fiscal deficit. Hence, the macroeconomic policy pursued in Denmark as of 1994 enlarged the scope of labour market policy choices; conversely, the labour market reform geared to increasing flexibility and the rate of employment widened the room for an expansionary, non-inflationary macroeconomic policy, and hence for economic growth. A virtuous circle was enacted.

It should be pointed out that the principles of macroeconomic stability, and hence prudent fiscal management, had been introduced in the late 1980s and strictly adhered to by the Government that took office in 1993. Macroeconomic stability is an essential dimension of the overall employment policy and a major explanatory variable of the positive labour market developments over the 1990s.

Two additional instruments need to be brought into the picture. One is monetary policy, which in Denmark used to be closely dependent on the level of interest rates in Germany, and now of the European Central Bank, and is therefore largely exogenous. The other is exchange rate policy, which has been slightly counter-cyclical, but within the limits allowed for by the exogenous monetary policy. By implication, fiscal policy is the only genuine macro-economic policy instrument available in Denmark, and the large but short-lived fiscal deficit spending applied in 1993 illustrates the proactive stance taken by the Government; the deficit was subsequently reduced and turned into a positive balance as of 1997. The competitive level of the real exchange rate as of 1994 significantly boosted exports up to the end of 1997, when a slight appreciation reduced the overheating of the economy. The high growth in exports played a significant role in generating employment after 1994. Overall, these macroeconomic conditions have sustained a period of high and non-inflationary growth with positive effects on employment and real wages.

The above considerations illustrate how dependent the Danish economy is on an adequate labour force. This is where the greatest threat may be seen in the future. Overall demographic growth will be of little help, as it is not projected to increase much beyond the annual rate of 0.4 per cent achieved over 1980–2000. By implication, given the age composition of the population, the labour force is expected to grow only marginally over the next 10–15 years. With employment to working-age population ratios already at a very high level, any increase on the supply side will have to come from a further reduction in unemployment, an increase in the employment ratios, particularly among workers aged 55 and over, or from immigration.

## Flexible enterprises and flexible work organization

Flexibility is a key dimension of management and work organization. The Nordic countries, including Denmark, recovered very rapidly following the crisis of the early 1990s, partly on the basis of extensive industrial and enterprise restructuring, and adoption of new technology and different patterns of work organization. A comparative study carried out by the Swedish National Board for Industrial and Technical Development (Nutek, 1999) on flexible work organization in enterprises in Denmark, Finland, Norway and Sweden substantiated the positive effects of the widespread practice of flexible work organization on productivity, employment growth and working conditions. Flexible work organization was identified as "functional" flexibility, based on decentralization of responsibility, extensive use of work teams and intensive skills development. The best-performing enterprises tend to be in sectors exposed to domestic or international competition, in financial, manufacturing and trade sectors with a definite edge for larger firms. It is not by coincidence that flexibility in work organization builds on two areas where Nordic countries have a long history of high-level performance, namely collective work relations and social dialogue between management and workers, and education and vocational training. The Nordic countries are high wage-cost countries and must therefore compete on the basis of quality products, high value added and high productivity. Flexible work organization, as opposed to what is usually referred to as labour market flexibility, provides an environment in which skills and knowledge can best be combined with autonomous decision-making within agreed parameters, in a safe and supportive working environment, all resulting in high labour productivity. Changing production patterns and greater custom design have relied extensively on this ability to organize work flexibly. Flexibility here should not be taken as opposed to security; rather it is the security of employment, levels of skills and working conditions that provide an environment conducive to an efficient and flexible use of the workforce. Promotion of the twin objectives of competitiveness and job satisfaction, security and welfare was already laid down in a Cooperation Agreement between the DA and the LO in 1989. The finding that trade unions and works councils can play a positive role in workplace changes is now also acknowledged by the OECD (1999).

The quest for better work organization and working conditions is apparent in the trade unions in Denmark and Sweden. In 1991, the Danish LO launched an initiative called "The Developing Workplace". It provides a vision of how work and workplaces should be designed, what the trade unions could do to attain better workplaces, and how this could contribute to the development of society as a whole. Quality products and services would be linked to a humane working environment that recognizes social and environmental responsibilities. Workplaces would have to be fashioned so as to further the personal development of the worker. To turn such convictions into reality, the LO developed a practical trade union strategy, including a toolkit for training for individual workplace development. Similarly in Sweden, the "Good Work" concept of the metalworkers' trade union reflects a search for an improved life resulting from the interaction of quality products, quality of working life and life outside the workplace. Specifically, the "Good Work" concept adheres to the following nine principles: employment security, fair profit-sharing, codetermination in enterprises, work organization for cooperation, professional competences for all employees, ongoing training, working hours oriented to social needs, equal opportunities and a safe working environment (Riegler, 2001).

Additionally, in Denmark there is evidence to suggest that, at least in some sectors, small enterprises are highly dynamic and innovative. Among the salient features are a high degree of organization, through which small firms collaborate extensively, e.g. in supply purchasing, product development and marketing, at the same time as they compete with each other on price and other dimensions. The innovativeness and flexible specialization of these firms rest largely on a skilled and adaptable workforce (Pyke and Sengenberger, 1992). Evidence suggests that craft training and decentralized education and training systems play a major role in the highly competitive small firms that account for a large proportion of growth in the private sector (Kristensen, 1992). In particular, entrepreneurial dynamism seems closely linked to craft-trained workers and small, family craft-oriented firms. These firms are embedded in a network of supportive institutions, which suggests again that small firm development, a high-risk venture, is intimately dependent on the institutional characteristics of their environment. Public services, infrastructure and representation all play an important role.

# The social foundations of decent work: A synthesis

In terms of GDP per capita, Denmark is among the five wealthiest countries in the industrialized world. Its economic fortune is not derived from natural wealth. Unlike countries such as the United States, Canada, Australia and Norway, Denmark does not dispose of large mineral resources. It owes its prosperity primarily to its high rate of employment and its high level of output for every hour of work put in by its workforce. The economic fruits are fairly equally distributed, and there are few people in Denmark who do not benefit. Although relative poverty is not unknown, its level is low by comparison with other countries.

Denmark also shows other signs of good economic health. Its economic performance can in large part be attributed to its social foundations – its institutions, actors and policies. Salient institutional features are: the effective collective organization of the labour market; the cooperation between employers and workers, who search together for commonly acceptable solutions to economic and social problems; a highly developed system of social protection; a large public sector providing social services and other public goods; an intriguing labour market policy, which is inspiring many others; efficient management of private and public enterprises; and finally, and most importantly, the ability of policy-makers to integrate the various social and economic policy components into a coherent whole. Denmark's learning and problem-solving capacity is enhanced by the fact that a relatively large number of its citizens participate in making and implementing decisions. The government and the public administration are decentralized, involving many local actors and allowing users to manage and administer public social services. Collective bargaining between workers and employers, which is probably more predominant and encompassing than anywhere else in the world, operates at various levels, and strongly motivates managers and worker representatives at the local level. All this adds up to mass mobilization of talent, knowledge and ideas, and an attitude of social responsibility that comes naturally when people are allowed and enabled to shape their own fortunes. It also reveals the ability of different parties – representing different and conflicting interests – to compromise, which nourishes Denmark's culture of collaboration and consensus. This spirit of compromise is visible not only in the realm of labour relations but also in public life in general. One historian has attributed the Danish ability to reach compromise solutions to a particular political constellation that has lasted throughout most of the twentieth century: no political party in Denmark has ever been able to win an absolute majority in the country. Hence, compromise became a necessity and a basic feature of Danish politics (Jespersen, 2001).

The Danish case demonstrates that decent work and economic strength support each other. While there may be trade-offs between the two, these can be managed through an appropriate policy mix. In Denmark, the two are largely congenial. Flexibility, equality, social security and broad social participation are explicit policy goals and, at the same time, instruments for problem-solving. Their combination allows the national economy to remain open to world markets, by strengthening the capacity to adjust rapidly to the changing global situation, and cushioning the negative effects of external economic shocks. Job loss and the ensuing unemployment are less disastrous for workers when, as in Denmark, unemployment compensation provides good income support, and public employment services efficiently assist in finding another job.

Denmark illustrates that large income transfers and, in particular, a high level of unemployment benefits need not act as a disincentive to gainful employment, and need not stifle the labour market, when combined with an extensive labour market policy that combines rights and obligations. Moreover, it demonstrates that flexibility need not be at the expense of security: the two can go hand in hand. It is worth emphasizing these points since many theorists and policy-makers have enunciated messages to the contrary. Apparently, there are ways of making the labour market flexible without dismantling social security. Workers who are adequately protected in case of redundancy tend to be more cooperative when it comes to structural change. As we have shown above, the Danish workers are the least fearful of job insecurity.

Furthermore, it is wrong to assume that a large public service sector will necessarily harm private business, crowd out investment or impede employment. The Danish case attests that the public sector and private business can be combined in a mutually beneficial partnership. Denmark's high level of employment is largely due to the expansion of female employment, which has been facilitated by comprehensive public care facilities for children and the elderly. Personal and social services have been a major source of female employment. In this regard, the continental European countries may have much to learn from the Nordic experience, when they attempt to reach the European Union targets for employment rates in general and for women in particular.

Another important lesson from Denmark is that it is not necessary to have extreme wage and income disparities for the labour market to function efficiently. Orthodox economists have argued that public or collective inter-ventions in the labour market, such as setting a minimum wage, compressing wage differentials or generating equality through social transfer payments, create distortions in the market and diminish allocative efficiency. Their view is that workers are discouraged from entering new occupations or sectors, or moving to locations of higher demand, because the wage structure does not provide the right price signals and sufficient incentives to move. This is valid only if it is assumed that wage differentials provide the only, or the best, mechanism for labour market clearing, and that sizeable wage increases are the only motive for working. Denmark shows that there is a viable alternative to the unfettered wage competition model of labour market flexibility, namely policies for continuous, comprehensive labour market training and other active measures that allow labour supply to be better matched to demand. Of course, this is costly: Denmark spends a considerable amount on income-compensating passive labour market policies, and it has one of the highest outlays on active labour market policies in the OECD. But the expenditure pays clear dividends, in human as well as in economic terms. The active approach enables the workforce to adapt to new job demands, without large-scale geographical mobility and the associated social uprooting. Moreover, not permitting large wage and income differentials means avoiding (relative) poverty at the lower end of the earnings scale. Thus, Denmark (and the other Nordic countries) has fewer working poor than the United States and other countries with large wage differentials, comparatively low minimum wages and less generous income replacement for redundant workers. A low incidence of poverty may not be the only reason for low rates of violence, crime and incarceration in the Nordic countries, but it is an important factor. Moreover, as was concluded in UNDP's *Human Development Report*, income inequality is likely to erode social capital, including the sense of trust and citizen responsibility that is key to the formation and sustainability of sound public institutions. It can undermine participation in such common spheres of community life as local sports leagues and parent–teacher associations. Inequality may be self-reinforcing, over time increasing the tolerance of inequality (UNDP, 2001).

Richard Freeman, a leading American labour economist, has pointed to the links between wage distribution, on the one hand, and hours of work, on the other. He posed the question why workers in the United States worked so many more hours than workers elsewhere. In fact, they have the highest average annual working hours in the OECD (1,833 hours in 1998 compared with 1,527 in Denmark). Freeman attributes this to comparatively weak trade unions, limited social security coverage and the need for workers in the large low-wage sector to work long hours to make up for low pay rates. One may also ask whether the very high incomes at the upper end of the earnings scale in the United States create incentives to work more. Lower working hours in Denmark and in other European countries have to be taken into account when appraising differences in real per capita disposable income between Europe and the United States. Prosperity in the United States is about 20 per cent higher than the European average, but this is almost entirely because of the extra hours worked. If average hours decline in accordance with preferences, "working less" represents as much of an income increase as "earning more" (Bell and Freeman, 1995; Schettkat, 2001). Danish workers seem to prefer fewer hours to more earnings. In 1994, 66 per cent of workers surveyed said that they preferred to work a shorter time for the same pay than have an increase in pay for the same hours; only 32 per cent expressed a preference for higher earnings. In 1985, the proportions had been 51 per cent and 38 per cent. Nowhere else in Europe was the choice so clearly in favour of fewer hours (OECD, 1998a).

Denmark has greatly benefited from the increasing consistency and effectiveness of its micro- and macroeconomic policies during the 1990s. A positive interaction has been secured between a controlled and well-timed macroeconomic policy, active labour market policies directed to flexibility and employability, the combination of employment flexibility with an incomes security policy for those unable to work or to find work, extensive social protection and access to low-cost social services enabling men and women to take up employment, and a policy of wage restraint based on coordinated and decentralized wage bargaining. Strong employers' and workers' organizations, and continuous dialogue with the government at both national and local levels, sustain this policy mix.

# CHALLENGES 3

Looking ahead, a number of important issues can readily be identified. From a minimalist perspective, the basic question is whether the Danish model described here can be sustained. The answer depends largely on the capacity of the Government and the social partners to maintain a rate of growth of the economy sufficient to ensure respectable growth in real incomes in conditions of macroeconomic stability and social cohesion. The most important constraint is labour supply, as very low population growth and an increasing proportion of elderly people will inexorably worsen the age dependency ratio, and erode the foundations of the Danish model. In a more ambitious perspective, Denmark needs to uphold its commitment to full employment in conditions of decent work for all women and men. These issues are considered in turn below.

## Maintaining welfare through adequate labour supply

The future economic growth and sustainability of the Danish welfare state depends, inter alia, on securing an adequate labour supply. A certain level of employment and productivity growth is essential for future growth and investment, as well as to produce the taxable income necessary to maintain the welfare services and entitlements. Total employment has grown slightly more rapidly than the labour force since 1989, as a result of rising rates of labour force participation and the massive reduction in unemployment. Only very moderate growth in the labour force is projected for the period up to 2010 (0.25 per cent per year), with employment increasing at a slightly higher rate (0.36 per cent per year). The first cause is low demographic growth, with total fertility rate currently at 1.7 live births per woman. This is higher than the very low European average, but below the minimum replacement level of 2.1 estimated by demographers to stabilize population in the long run. Second, the employment to working-age population ratio is already comparatively high, and very close to the historical and sociodemographic limit of around 80 per cent (the highest rate is currently in Norway at 78.0 per cent) (Ministry of Finance, 2001).

Nevertheless, a number of areas can readily be identified in which potential labour supply could be turned into effective labour supply. One such area is in the 55–64 age group. The Government and the social partners agreed in 1999 to reverse the policy, adopted in 1979, of encouraging early retirement. Incentives are now given to workers to stay in the labour market beyond age 60, and to postpone early retirement until at least 62 years of age. Early retirement was in tune with the labour market of the 1980s, which was marked by high unemployment, but has proven increasingly anachronistic as unemployment has decreased. A reasonable objective would be to raise the employment rate of workers aged 55–64 years from the present 54 per cent to, say, 60 per cent (which would still be below the level in Sweden) within a few years. The employment rates of workers aged up to 59 years have been rising lately, but those of workers aged 60 and over remain comparatively low. It is here that efforts should be concentrated.

Another measure would be to seek to lower unemployment even further; moving from 5.0 per cent unemployment to, say, 3.0 per cent represents a gain of approximately 60,000 persons. A more promising area would be to continue active labour market policies, and to enlarge their scope of application to include beneficiaries of transfers other than unemployment benefits. This would include persons who would have been interested by one of the previous early retirement schemes (now reformed or closed), as well as people on extended sick leave, invalidity pension or other social assistance. It is likely that these groups will have lower employability than the temporarily unemployed, and hence will need more finely tuned measures to help them return to employment. Labour market policy instruments may need to be revised. In all these areas, taxation policy is likely to have a direct influence on labour market participation, and should be reviewed in that light. Finally, in view of the inevitable need to rely on a greater proportion of immigrant labour in the future, Denmark should continue to evaluate the labour market advantages and potential costs of immigration. Gradual initiatives in all these areas are likely to be sufficient to bridge the projected gap between demand and supply of labour up to 2010–15. Beyond that, when the labour force starts to decline in absolute terms, such measures will probably not be sufficient. Nevertheless, the range and depth of possible measures aimed at maintaining an adequate supply of labour are considerable, and Denmark should be able to come up with innovative and practical ideas through intensive social dialogue.

# Sustaining flexicurity in the labour market

Several challenges and new opportunities confront Denmark's labour market policy of combining flexibility with security. It is already sometimes difficult to find enough labour market measures to fulfil the right of every unemployed person to activation. As a result, the period of passive receipt of benefit between activation measures has had to be prolonged. The problem may be aggravated in a future recession. Will the activation policy be effective in a period of lower demand? Will there be enough activation slots for all unemployed people? And especially, will there be enough jobs or training slots of adequate quality?

A considerable number of non-employed persons receive transfer payments (amounting to nearly 23 per cent of the population aged 15–66 years), with the biggest components relating to early retirement (5.0 per cent), sickness and social problems (4.1 per cent) and disability (7.4 per cent) (Callesen, 2000b). Although this is clearly a feature of developed welfare states – in this regard Denmark is below or on a par with all other Nordic countries except Iceland – it remains to be seen whether the existing proportion of the population that is inactive is sustainable. Again, in the event of an economic downturn, there is bound to be increased pressure on state budgets. If the supply-side restrictions linked to ageing of the workforce continue, the pressures to activate some of this potential will increase. In fact, both pressures call for a continuation of the activation strategy, with a view to creating more non-subsidized market jobs.

There is also a question about responsibility for future security of employment. At present, it is relatively easy for an employer to terminate an employment contract. It is also not very costly, because there are only two "waiting days", which have to be covered by the employer, before the person is entitled to compensation from the public unemployment fund. This regulation provides few incentives for avoiding lay-offs, and tends to encourage enterprises to make adjustments first by reducing the number of employees. The social responsibility of employers may therefore be lower than in labour markets with stricter regulations on employment protection. This may be one reason why trade unions are suggesting an additional three waiting days before unemployment compensation becomes effective, as a means of reducing lay-offs and unemployment. A detailed analysis of the costs and benefits associated with dismissal would be useful to promote a more balanced distribution between employers, employees and the unemployment insurance fund. Additionally, the consequences of the high job turnover for productivity are not very clear. The social partners might look at alternative models of cost-sharing, such as the experience-rating of the unemployment insurance scheme in the United States, or the short-term working schemes in Europe.

There would also appear to be new opportunities to further develop some elements of the active labour market policy. For example, job rotation has generally been practised in large companies and in the public sector. There should be possibilities to extend this instrument to small and medium-sized enterprises.

## Achieving full employment

Denmark is committed to a policy of full employment. But what is full employment? Should one accept that the current unemployment rate of 4.7 per cent (OECD standardized value for 2000) is close to the minimum compatible with stable inflation, and that a further reduction would unleash inflationary wage pressures? Or should one restate the Beveridge definition of 1944 of full employment as a labour market in which there are slightly more unfilled vacancies than unemployed persons, with available jobs being acceptable and fair in terms of wages, location and type. Such full employment is compatible with a certain level of frictional unemployment, defined – also by Beveridge – as the normal lag between losing one job and finding another. This level of unemployment is usually estimated at between 2 and 4 per cent, which was the level registered in Denmark during the 1950s and 1960s when unemployment was low in Europe generally. Data for the first quarter of 2001 indicate that several European countries are experiencing very low unemployment rates, among them the Netherlands (1.8 per cent, but with strong wage inflationary pressures as labour demand outpaces supply), Switzerland (1.6 per cent), and Austria (2.7 per cent). The latter two countries seem to be able to combine low unemployment with low and stable inflation. In the United States, unemployment has fallen below 5 per cent since 1997 without serious inflationary pressures, even though the rate of unemployment compatible with stable inflation had been estimated at much higher levels. Denmark should be able to achieve and sustain full employment, as defined by Beveridge, with an unemployment rate close to 3 per cent. This would imply further reductions in long-term unemployment, as well as further lowering of the average duration of periods of unemployment. This should be possible, as has been pointed out earlier, without lowering the level of unemployment benefits or increasing wage dispersion. It could also imply, as mentioned above, increasing the disincentives to employers to lay off workers.

## Full employment and decent work

It should be stressed that full employment can only be achieved and sustained if the Beveridge conditions recalled above (jobs with acceptable conditions of pay, type and location) are fully reinterpreted in the context of the labour market conditions prevailing in Denmark today. The employment to be generated should be highly skilled, conform to the highest standards of working conditions and ensure high productivity. Three major areas are worthy of mention. First, working conditions should be continuously reviewed and improved, in particular in relation to specific age groups, such as workers aged 55 and above, and to occupational safety and health. New concerns have recently emerged around the as yet ill-defined notion of stress, referring to a complex set of factors related to physical and mental duress at the workplace. In fact stress, and absences associated with stress, have become a major concern for the social partners and the Government. This issue has also been placed high on the policy agenda of the Nordic Council of Ministers. The modalities of worker participation in enterprises should also be kept under review, as areas for the direct involvement of workers and union representatives expand or change.

Second, despite the considerable progress achieved in Denmark, gender equality and equality of opportunity are still an unfinished business. Differences remain in pay, in occupational patterns, and in qualifications and skills. Women entrepreneurs are rare. Some of the differences may reflect elements of discrimination, while in other areas patterns of social segregation prevail. The objective is not to aim for total elimination of occupational or sectoral segregation by sex, but rather to ensure equality of opportunity in the labour market based upon freedom of choice. This would further enhance flexibility in the labour market and mitigate supply bottlenecks. Denmark has come a long way towards socializing the costs of child-rearing and it is important to continue to improve opportunities for young parents, and particularly young mothers, to combine family and work.

Third, Denmark is likely to see the proportion of immigrants in the labour force rise from 5 per cent at present to a predicted 7–8 per cent in 2010. This will reflect both a rising number of immigrants in the working-age population and higher rates of labour force participation. This development presents both a challenge and a partial solution to the ageing of the population. At present, the employment rates of immigrants are lower and their unemployment rates higher than those of the native labour force, partly because of lack of skills and language proficiency. Targeted measures to facilitate immigrants' integration and enhance their employability are being implemented. Since 1999, for instance, municipalities must offer an introduction programme, for a period of three years, that includes courses in the Danish language and Danish society, as well as activation measures involving employment experience, training or education. The Government, together with the social partners, the Council of Immigrants, a network of ethnic consultants, and the Board of Ethnic Equality, has drawn up an action plan and adopted various measures to facilitate the access of people of different ethnic origins to the labour market. These integration measures have the potential not only to improve equality in the labour market, but also to ease supply shortages. In spite of the many social and cultural problems linked to immigration in many – but not all – countries, it should be considered as a serious option. A policy of organized flows of migrant labour, possibly in the context of the current enlargement policy of the European Union, could be considered.

## Labour market implications of an ageing workforce

The proportion of the population aged 64 and above is predicted to rise from 15 per cent in 2000 to over 20 per cent by 2030. The proportion of the working-age population (15–64 years) is expected to drop from approximately 67 per cent to 63 per cent, with a corresponding increase in the economic dependency ratio (number of inactive people per 100 active people) from 81 in 2000 to 93 in 2010. The financial burden on the active population will increase under the combined pressures of a higher total pension burden and a greater demand for health and care services, which will strain taxation and fiscal outlays. While the speed of change is extremely rapid in historical terms, there is nevertheless sufficient time to design policies to mitigate the adverse consequences. In particular, measures to raise the effective retirement age closer to the statutory age are a priority. This would imply a complete reversal of the earlier policy, from financial incentives to retire early to incentives to retire later. In policy terms, simply removing incentives to early retirement is not the same as encouraging workers to retire later. This will require measures addressing both public health matters and working conditions. It is important for Denmark to pursue efforts to raise the relatively low average life expectancy in the country (76.1 years in 1999 compared with 79.6 and 80.8 years in Sweden and Japan). This is a public health matter related to nutrition, social habits and quality of health services, as well as an occupational health issue. In particular, further improvements are needed in the working conditions of older workers in aspects such as distribution of tasks, special working-time arrangements and training opportunities, e.g. in the use of new technology and computer literacy. The possibility of a more flexible exit from the labour market for older workers, e.g. through part-time jobs combined with semi-retirement, should be envisaged. Information campaigns are needed to dispel the notion that older workers are less productive, when they are most often experienced and knowledgeable.

## High growth in labour productivity

Sustaining high levels of GDP per capita, and hence of welfare entitlements, will inevitably rest on achieving high rates of growth of labour and total productivity.

Growth of labour productivity accelerated in the 1990s to above 3 per cent per year. Current projections suggest that labour productivity will increase at around half that rate (1.7 per cent per year on average) over the next 10 to 20 years. A number of structural features in the Danish economy (large number of small firms, large public sector, manufacturing output dominated by consumer goods rather than intermediate goods) may hold down the growth. Still, investments should be made to expand high-value-added goods and services on the basis of the existing high quality of infrastructure, services, education and skills of the labour force. A high level of investment in areas that sustain high growth of labour productivity should continue to be encouraged. This would compensate somewhat for the expected moderate growth in employment because of demographic factors, and help sustain a high rate of GDP growth. Work organization, worker participation and working conditions all have a direct bearing on labour productivity. Denmark's positive experience in these areas should be pursued, possibly with greater attention to the social costs related to work performed under tight schedules.

## Taxation and labour supply

A standard criticism of welfare states is that the high average and marginal tax rates required to finance benefits (except in countries with high-value natural resources) stifle the incentive to work and hence reduce employment. This has not been the experience in Denmark. The country is not facing a problem of low pay. In fact, low-wage earners represent less than 10 per cent of total employ-ment and are mostly part-time young workers (often combining work and studies). In addition, the very low payroll contributions and the highly pro-gressive income taxation have maintained a positive income differential between full-time work at or around the minimum wage and unemployment benefits. Recently enacted reforms aim to increase that differential. Hence, "make work pay" policies do not apply in the same way as they might in other countries. Nevertheless, one could imagine that high unemployment income replacement rates, favourable early retirement benefits and high average income tax rates could discourage people from active job search. On the one hand, tax reforms negotiated under the so-called Whitsun agreement, and implemented progres-sively over the 1999–2002 period, provide for lower marginal tax rates for low-income workers. On the other hand, better-focused and more decentralized active labour market measures play an important role. Rather than with low-wage earners or the unemployed, the problem lies with early retirement schemes, which have been enormously popular, particularly among less-skilled workers. The attractiveness of this option has now been reduced, but still financial incentives to retire later will have to be accompanied by improved working conditions for older people. A similar problem may lie with average and higher-income earners with regard to working hours, when the marginal gain from working additional hours is fully eroded by the higher marginal income tax rate. Although the demand for shorter working hours is fairly widespread in line with a European lifestyle aspiration, part of the motivation may be linked to tax rates. This is an issue that the social partners may want to address in greater detail, as further reductions in working time would have to be weighed against the need to finance welfare benefits within acceptable taxation levels.

# Denmark in the European Union

Four issues are considered here. First, the harmonization of EU policies is based on Directives adopted by the European Council, as well as other types of regulations, benchmarking and coordination methods. This can be at odds with the Danish preference for policy-making based on extensive consultations between the social partners and with the Government, which often leads to more informal agreements. The difference lies much more in form and procedures than with the contents of decisions. Is there a way of reconciling these two approaches? The social partners are closely consulted on all aspects of EU policy in Denmark, but their role in the national implementation of a European Directive will necessarily be distinct from an agreement negotiated directly with them. The participation of employer and worker representatives at the EU level can complement, but is no substitute for, participation at the national level.

Second, how is Denmark likely to be affected by the enlargement of the European Union? It is unlikely that Denmark's exports will suffer much from increased competition, although some losses in agriculture cannot be ruled out; rather Denmark may gain from greater market access. With regard to the labour market, it is debatable whether Denmark will gain from an inflow of skilled labour, or lose from an inflow of unskilled labour and an outflow of skilled workers. Even if a transitional period for the free movement of labour is decided upon, as some Member States have already suggested, the tight labour market in Denmark requires that this issue is addressed and debated. More organized flows of immigrant labour and better labour market information regarding the occupational and skills profile of vacancies could be beneficial.

Third, although Denmark is not a member of the EMU, any asymmetric economic shock in one major trading partner country or in Denmark itself, which would not necessarily be reflected in an adjustment in the monetary policy of the European Central Bank, could entail negative economic and labour market consequences. In principle, the question need not arise, since Denmark has decided to retain its monetary autonomy. In practice, monetary policy in Denmark, for obvious reasons, closely follows decisions of the ECB. In fact, Denmark has pursued a fixed exchange rate regime for almost 20 years, and the Danish crown has been tied to the euro since 1999. The remarkable stability of the economy can be linked to fiscal and structural policies. Fiscal policy has played its traditional counter-cyclical role, and maintaining a solid surplus has been a concern of the Government in order to reduce debt obligations and retain such fiscal capacity. But depending on the depth and duration of an exogenous shock, such a policy may quickly reach a limit. A second lever has been structural policies, in the labour market and social protection, as well as social dialogue and the ability to strike wage agreements that are coherent with the prevailing economic cycle and with forecasts. This capacity is enhanced by the credibility of the fixed exchange rate regime ensuring low interest rates in Denmark. Another means of transmission of an exogenous shock could be through long-term interest rates, which would directly affect yields on mortgage-credit bonds. Most Danish households own and finance their housing, the cost of which directly affects income and consumption levels. Rising mortgage interest rates, for any reason external to Denmark, would certainly fuel strong demands for wage adjustments, and these could threaten future growth prospects.

Finally, there is the issue of tax competition and tax harmonization. Low corporate taxes and low payroll taxes put Denmark at an advantage in the European common market. Conversely, high income taxes and relatively high indirect taxes put it at a disadvantage. Since income taxation is steeply progressive in Denmark, with relatively high marginal tax rates, high-wage and high-income earners may opt to migrate to countries with lower rates of income tax.. This is highly debatable, as the net cost of welfare benefits and entitlements may well outweigh the benefits of lower income tax. Nevertheless, Denmark would stand to gain from measures towards greater tax harmonization in the European Union, which would tend to reduce the perceived advantages of existing tax havens (for a recent discussion of the impact of EU membership on the Nordic welfare state, see Kiander, 2001).

Each of these issues poses critical policy challenges. EU membership has been a divisive issue, splitting the population into two camps of approximately equal size.

## Strong institutions and social dialogue

As has been pointed out, strong institutions, in particular social dialogue, are a defining characteristic of Denmark, and explain to a large extent the remarkable achievements recorded over the 1990s and even earlier. It can be surmised that these will also provide the means to deal with the challenges that now loom over the future, to sustain the high levels of GDP per capita, welfare benefits, gender equality and social cohesion described earlier. Many of the challenges to be faced lie at the core of labour and social policy issues. The capacity of the social partners to agree on wage adjustments that are compatible with stable inflation, social aspirations and international competitiveness stands out as critical. The social partners and with them the Government are ideally placed to pursue a practice that has delivered good results in the past. As in the past, innovative and pragmatic policy responses adapted to the case at hand can be found.

# BIBLIOGRAPHY

Adema, Willem. 2001. *Net social expenditure, labour market and social policy*. Occasional Papers, No. 52 (Paris, OECD).

Anxo, Dominique; Flood, Lenard; Rubery, Jill. 1999. *Household income distribution and working time patterns: An international comparison*, working paper (Gelsenkirchen, Institut Arbeit und Technik).

Auer, Peter. 2000. *Employment revival in Europe: Labour market success in Austria, Denmark, Ireland and the Netherlands* (Geneva, ILO).

— (ed.). 2001. *Changing labour markets in Europe: The role of institutions and policies* (Geneva, ILO).

Bell, L.; Freeman, R. B. 1995. "Why do Americans and Germans work different hours?", in Buttler, F. et al. (eds.): *Institutional frameworks and labour market performance: Comparative views on the US and German economies.* (London and New York, Routledge).

Bosch, Gerhard. 2001. "Working time: From redistribution to modernisation", in Auer (ed.), 2001.

Buck, Ingerlise. 2000. "Spielregeln der dänischen Arbeitnehmerkapitalisten", in *Die Mitbestimmung* (Düsseldorf), No. 11, p. 47.

Bureau of Labor Statistics. 2000a. *International comparisons of hourly compensation costs for production workers in manufacturing, 2000* (Washington, DC, US Department of Labor) (http://www.bls.gov/fls/).

—. 2000b. *Comparative real gross domestic product per capita and per employed person, 1960–1998* (Washington, DC, US Department of Labor) (http://www.bls.gov/fls/).

Callesen, Per. 2000a. "Active and preventive approaches: A note based on the recent Danish experience", in *Policies towards full employment* (Paris, OECD).

—. 2000b. *Incentives and disincentives to work: Unemployment insurance and early retirement – key issues*, paper presented at the Workshop on Labour Markets, Brussels, 26–27 Oct.

Calmfors, L.; Driffill, J. 1993. *Centralisation of wage bargaining and macroeconomic performance: A survey*, Economic Working Paper, No. 131 (Paris, OECD).

CEDEFOP. 1994. *Le système de formation professionnelle au Danemark* (Luxembourg) .

DA. 2001. *Labour market report 2001*, English summary (Copenhagen).

Danish Government. 2000. *Structural monitoring – International benchmarking of Denmark*, English version (Copenhagen).

Ebbinghaus, B.; Visser, J. 2000. *Trade unions in Western Europe since 1945* (London and New York, Macmillan).

Economist Intelligence Unit. 2001. *Country forecast: Denmark* (London).

Esping-Andersen, Gösta. 1990. *The three worlds of welfare capitalism* (London, Polity Press).

— (ed.). 1996. *Welfare states in transition: National adaptations in global economies* (London, Sage).

European Commission. 2001. *Employment in Europe 2001 – recent trends and prospects* (Brussels, Employment and Social Affairs Unit).

European Foundation for the Improvement of Living and Working Conditions. 2001. *Third European Survey on Working Conditions 2000* (Dublin).

EIROnline (European Industrial Relations Observatory) (http://217.141.24.196/).

Eurostat. 2001. *European social statistics – labour force survey results 2000* (Luxembourg, European Communities).

Eurostat; European Commission. 2001. *The social situation in the European Union* (Luxembourg).

Gabriel, Phyllis; Liimatainen, Marjo-Riitta. 2000. *Mental health in the workplace: Introduction* (Geneva, ILO).

Greve, Bent. 2000. "Aktive Arbeitsmarktpolitik in Dänemark – Realität oder Rhetorik?", in *WSI-Mitteilungen*, Vol. 53, May (Frankfurt/Main).

ILO. 1997. *World Labour Report 1997–98: Industrial relations, democracy and social stability* (Geneva).

—. 1999. *Decent work*, Report of the Director-General, International Labour Conference, 87th Session (Geneva).

—. 2000. *World Labour Report 2000: Income security and social protection in a changing world* (Geneva).

—. 2001a. *Yearbook of Labour Statistics 2000* (Geneva).

—. 2001b. *World Employment Report: Life at work in the information economy* (Geneva).

—. 2001c. *Reducing the decent work deficit – A global challenge.* Report of the Director-General, International Labour Conference, 89th Session (Geneva).

—. 2002. *Key Indicators of the Labour Market* (Geneva).

IMF. 2000. *International Financial Statistics Yearbook* (Washington, DC).

—. 2001. *World Economic Outlook,* May (Washington, DC).

Jacobsen, Per.; Hasselbach, Ole. 1998. "Denmark", in Blanpain, R. (ed.): *International encyclopedia for labour law and industrial relations* (The Hague, London, Kluwer Law International), Vol. 5.

Jespersen, Knud, J. V. 2001. *Factsheet Denmark* (Copenhagen, Royal Danish Ministry of Foreign Affairs).

Jorgensen, Carsten. 2001. *EU part-time work directive implemented through new "dual" method*, EIROnline, p. 98, June.

Kiander, Jaakko. 2001. *The future of the Nordic welfare model*, unpublished paper (Geneva, ILO).

Kristensen, Peer Hull. 1992. "Industrial districts in West Jutland", in Pyke, F. and Sengenberger, W. (eds.): *Industrial districts and local economic regeneration* (Geneva, International Institute for Labour Studies).

Kruppe, T. 2001. *Assessing labour market dynamics: European evidence*, Employment Papers, No. 15 (Geneva, ILO).

Larsson, Allan. 1999. *The European employment strategy towards the Helsinki summit*, unpublished paper (Luxembourg, European Commission).

Lind, Jens. 2000. "Recent issues on the social pact in Denmark", in Fajertag, G. and Pochet, P. (eds.): *Social pacts in Europe, new dynamics* (Brussels, European Trade Union Institute).

LO. 2000a. *LO-Dokumentation*, No. 2.

—. 2000b. *Labour markets in the EU* (Copenhagen).

—. 2001. *Danish Labour News*, March, No. 4.

Lönnroth, Juhani. 2000. "Active labour market policies: Continuity and change", in OECD: *Policies towards full employment* (Paris).

Maddison, Angus. 1995. *Monitoring the world economy 1820–1992* (Paris, OECD).

Madsen, Jorgen Steen. 2000. *"Danish model" maintained by implementation of EU directives through collective agreements*, EIROnline, January.

—; Jorgensen, Carsten; Due, Jesper. 2000. "Collective bargaining in Europe – 1999–2000: Denmark", in Fajertag, G. (ed.): *Collective bargaining in Europe 1998–99* (Brussels, European Trade Union Institute).

Madsen, Per Kongshoj. 2001. *Employment protection and labour market policies: Trade-offs and complementarities: The case of Denmark*, Employment Papers, 2001/21 (Geneva, ILO).

Melkas, Helina; Anker, Richard. 1998. *Gender equality and occupational segregation in Nordic labour markets* (Geneva, ILO).

Ministry of Finance. 2001. *The Danish economy 2001* (Copenhagen, Danish Government) (http://www.fm.dk).

Nordic Council. 2000. *Supply of labour in the Nordic countries, experience, developments and political deliberations.* Report by a Committee of Nordic civil servants, No. 21 (Copenhagen).

North, Douglas. 1990. *Institutions, institutional change and economic performance* (Cambridge, Cambridge University Press).

Nutek (Swedish National Board for Industrial and Technical Development). 1999. *Flexibility matters: Flexible enterprises in the Nordic countries* (Stockholm).

OECD. 1997. *Employment Outlook* (Paris).

—. 1998a. *Employment Outlook*. (Paris).

—. 1998b. *Tax/benefit position of employees* (Paris).

—. 1998c. *Pathways and participation in vocational and technical education and training* (Paris).

—. 1998d. *Health outcomes in OECD countries. A framework of health indicators for outcome oriented policy-making* (Paris).

—. 1999. *Employment Outlook* (Paris).

—. 2000a. *Historical Statistics* (Paris).

—. 2000b. *Labour Force Statistics* (Paris).

—. 2000c. *Revenue Statistics* (Paris).

—. 2000d. *Small and Medium Enterprise Outlook* (Paris).

—. 2000e. *Literacy in the information age* (Paris).

—. 2001a. *Employment Outlook* (Paris).

—. 2001b. *Education at a Glance* (Paris).

—. 2001c. *Economic Outlook* (Paris).

—. 2001d. *Education Policy Analysis* (Paris).

OECD; European Commission; Government of Finland. 2000. *Policies towards full employment*, Proceedings of an International Conference, Helsinki (Paris).

Palme, Joakim. 1999. *The Nordic mode and the modernisation of social protection in Europe* (Copenhagen, Nordic Council of Ministers).

Petersen, Kare. 1997. *Do collective agreements ensure full coverage and compliance with EU directives?* EIROnline, October.

Plantenga, Jannebe; Hansen, Johan. 1999. "Assessing equal opportunities in the European Union", in *International Labour Review*, Vol. 138, No. 4.

Pyke, F.; Sengenberger, W. (eds.). 1992. *Industrial districts and local economic regeneration* (Geneva, International Institute for Labour Studies).

Riegler, Claudius H. 2001. *"Good work" in Sweden: Concept and practice*, unpublished document (Geneva, ILO).

Rubery, Jill. 2001. "Equal opportunities and employment policy", in Auer (ed.), 2001.

Scarpetta, S.; Bassanini, A.; Pilat, D.; Schreyer, P. 2000. *Economic growth in the OECD area: Recent trends at the aggregate and sectoral level* (Paris, OECD).

Scharpf, Fritz. 2000. "Der globale Sozialstaat", in *Die Zeit*, No. 24.

Schettkat, Ronald. 2001. "Small economy macro-economics", in Auer (ed.), 2001.

Singh, Ajit. 1995. "Institutional requirements for full employment in advanced economies", in *International Labour Review*, Vol. 143, No. 4–5.

Statistics Denmark (http://www.dst.dk), various years.

Stephens, John. 1996. "The Scandinavian Welfare States: Achievements, crisis and prospects", in Esping-Andersen (ed.), 1990.

Streeck, Wolfgang; Schmitter, Philippe C. 1985. "Community, market, state – and associations?", in *European Sociological Review* (Oxford University Press), Vol. 1, No. 2, September.

Tiainen, Pekka. 1999. "Employment and welfare in Finland in the years 1860–2030", in *Labour Policy Study* (Helsinki, Ministry of Labour), No. 211, p. 21.

Traxler, Franz; Kittel, Bernhard. 2000. *The bargaining structure, its context, and performance*, unpublished paper prepared for the Conference on Economic Internationalization and Democracy, University of Vienna, 14–15 December.

UNDP. 2001. *Human Development Report 2001* (New York and Oxford, Oxford University Press).

Visser, Jelle. 2001. "Industrial relations and social dialogue", in Auer (ed.), 2001.

World Bank. 2000. *World Development Indicators* (Washington, DC).

World Economic Forum. 2001. *Global Competitiveness Report 2000* (New York, Oxford University Press).

# INDEX

Note: Page numbers in bold refer to tables; those in italic refer to figures.

Abolition of Forced Labour Convention, 1957 (No. 105) 27
"activation" into labour market 73, 74, 89
agriculture, cooperative movements 45
Amsterdam, Treaty of 3
annual leave, paid 10, 53, 77
annual working hours 10, *16*, 77
Apprenticeship Act (1956) 72
apprenticeship scheme 49
Arbitration Boards 53
Australia 22
Austria xi, 8, 77, 90
   GDP per capita **75**
   income distribution 11, 26
   social dialogue *29*
   working hours 10, *16*

Basic Vocational Education Act (1977) 72
Belgium 28, 59, 69
   GDP per capita **75**
   income 11, 26
   labour productivity 30, 77
benefits 21, 56, 77, 89
   conditional on active labour market participation 56, 61, 73–4
   duration of payment 19, 21, 73
   passive 83, 89
   percentage distribution **20**
   targeted 56
   unemployment 19, 56, 60–1, 83

Beveridge, Sir William, definition of full employment 90
birth rate 87
Board of Ethnic Quality 91–2
bureaucracy, satisfaction with 35
business environment 33, 35, 60, 81
   small and medium-sized businesses 45, 46, 77
business start-ups 35

Canada 28, 77
   GDP per capita **75**
child benefits 21, 56
childcare
   leave 21
   public 64, 83, 91
Clean Working Environment 2005 action plan 55–6
Climate Agreement (1999) 50
collective action 28–9, 80
collective agreements 46
   coverage 29, *29*, 53–4
   duration 48, 53
   framework agreements 50
   minimum wage 11, 18
collective bargaining 28, 40, 46, 47–9, 82
   decentralized 48
   origins of 49–50
   preferred to legislation 27, 40, 46, 53–4
   wage bargaining 50–3
   *see also* social dialogue

collective organization 28, 46, 80, 82
  *see also* trade unions
communication technology 35
competitiveness 33, 35, 80
  factor in wage bargaining 51
  international 80, 82
Confederation of White-Collar and Crown
  Servants (FTF) 47
consensus 82
consumer prices **37**
Copenhagen Declaration on Social Development
  and Programme of Action vi, xi
corporatism, associative 47
corruption 60
Council of Immigrants 91–2
craft and guild organization 45
craft training 81
crime rates 60, 77, 84

Danish Confederation of Employers (DA) 29, 47
  Cooperation Agreement 80
  minimum wage 18
Danish Confederation of Graduate Employee
  Associations (CA) 47
Danish Confederation of Trade Unions (LO)
  29, 47
  Cooperation Agreement 80
day care 56
decent work
  Danish agenda 1–3
  and full employment 90–2
  indicators 6–30
  social foundations 81–5
  *see also* labour market policies; social
    protection
decentralization
  of decision-making 47–8
  education and training 81
  political 45
  wage bargaining 51
  and work flexibility 80
decision-making, decentralized 47–8
democracy 45, 46

workplace 49
demographic trends 79–80, 87, 92
  *see also* older workers
Denmark
  Decent Work agenda vi, xi, 1–3
  economic and social indicators 30-3, *34,
    37, 75*
  future sustainability 2–3, 78–80, 87–96
  "Golden Age" (1950-73) 1–2, 35
  institutional model 45
  policy choices 1, 43
  welfare state model 44, 56–62
  *see also* subject headings
disability benefits 21, 56, 89
Discrimination (Employment and Occupation)
  Convention, 1958 (No. 111) 27
drug and alcohol addiction 56
"dual-earner" model 62
early retirement 22, 77, 89, 93–4
  flexible 92
  pensions 21, 56
  policy reverse 88
economic growth 31, 40–1, 75, 78, 87
  *see also* labour productivity; macroeconomics
economic performance indicators 30–5, **34,
  37,** 38
Economist Intelligence unit (EIU) 33
economy
  macroeconomic and microeconomic policy
    interaction 75–80, 85
  open 45, 60
  structural changes 61, 82
education 39, 41, 60
  gender equality 23
  high school movement 46
  public expenditure on 9, 77
  tertiary 9, *15*, 72
  upper secondary 9, *15*, 72
  and vocational training 49, 72
elderly (dependent)
  care 56, 64, 83
  *see also* older workers
employees *see* workers

employer organizations 29, 85
employers
  social responsibility 89
  social security contributions 20, 22, 58–9, 61
employment
  conditions for full employment 90–2
  full employment policy 90
  informal 62
  job creation 89
  job satisfaction 80
  mobility 67–70
  protection measures 19–20, 39, 66, 89
  security of 73, 80, 83, 89
  turnover rate 89
  *see also* employment rate; labour market;
    unemployment
Employment Policy Convention, 1964 (No. 122)
  27
employment to population ratio 6, **75**, 76, **76**, 87
employment rate 6–7, *12*, 38, 62, 81
  men 6
  older workers 7, 77
  women 6, 24, 62, 76
  young people 6, 76
Equal Remuneration Convention, 1951 (No. 100)
  27
equality
  of opportunity 91
  *see also* gender equality
ethnic minorities 91–2
  *see also* immigrants
European Central Bank 79, 94–5
European Commission
  and Danish implementation of Directives
    54, 94
  Directive on Part-time Work 54
  Directive on Working Time (1993) 54
European Community Household Panel 41
European Council 3, 6

European Economic Community 36
European Foundation for the Improvement of
  Living and Working Conditions 5
European Monetary System 36

European Monetary Union (EMU) 44
European Union (EU) 5, 44
  collective agreements *29*
  Danish membership of 95
  economic and social indicators 30-33, *34*,
    35-36, 38, 42
  education and training 9, *15*
  employment rate 6-7, 12, *13*
  Employment Strategy 3
  enlargement 92, 94
  gender equality 24, 26, 27
  Jobs Summit (Luxembourg 1997) 3
  labour force participation 6, *12*
  occupational safety and health 19
  social security 19-22, *23*
  tax harmonization 95
  trade unions 28, 29, *29*
  Treaty of Amsterdam 3
  unemployment and inactivity 8, 9, *14, 15, 70*
  wages and income 11, *17*
  working hours 10, *16*
Eurostat 5
exchange rate policy 79, 95

family and work balance
  provisions for 21, 63–4
  *see also* gender equality; women;
    working hours
Finland 9, 19, 32, 70
  and EU 44
  income and earnings 11, 26, 64
  public social security expenditure 22
  social dialogue *29*
  unemployment 9, 19, 69
  work organization 28, 35, 80
fiscal balance 33, 78–9
fiscal policy, independence of 79, 95
fixed-term employment 7
flexibility 45, 74, 80, 85
  management and work organization 80–1
Forced Labour Convention, 1930 (No. 29) 27
foreigners
  employment opportunities 73

unemployment 8
*see also* immigrants
framework agreements 50
France 10, 28, 61, 73
    employment rate **76**
    GDP per capita **75**
    labour productivity 77
    public social security expenditure 22, 58, 59
    social dialogue *29*
    wages 18, 26
freedom of association 27–8
Freedom of Association and Protection of the
    Right to Organise Convention, 1948
    (No. 87) 27
Freeman, Richard 84
fundamental rights 27–8, 40

GDP
    labour productivity rates 30, 41, 77, 81, 92–3
    per capita 30–1, *36*, **37**, 75–6, **75**
gender equality 23–7, 40, 91
    Anglo-Saxon model 63–4
    "dual-earner" model 62–4, 77
    education 23
    employment rate 24, 76
    labour force participation 23–4, 65–6
    male-breadwinner model 63
    occupational segregation 24–6, *25*, **25**, 40,
        64–5
    wages 26, *26*, 65
    and welfare policy 62–5
    *see also* women
Germany 10, 21, 35, 64
    economic and social indicators 30, 35, **37**,
        **75**, 77
    education *15*
    employment rate **76**
    public social security expenditure 58, 59
    relative poverty 18
    structural unemployment 69
    taxation 32
    wages 10, 51, **52**
Gini index, of income distribution 11

Global Competitiveness Report (2000) 35
Good Work concept (Sweden) 81
government *see* State
Greece 7, 67

health care 56, 92
    *see also* occupational safety and health
health problems, work-related 18–19
hourly earnings *17*, 51, **52**
    nominal 10–11
households
    dual earning 62–4, 77
    single adult 77
housing
    allowances 56
    ownership rates 95

Iceland 9
immigrants
    integration of 73, 91
    and labour market needs 88, 94
    unemployment 39
imprisonment rates 60, 77, 84
inactivity (employment) 8–9, *15*
inclusion, welfare model 56
income
    low 11
    real disposable (per capita) 84
income distribution 11, *17*, 81–2
income (in)equality 11, 39, 84
income redistribution 56, 59
income replacement rates **20**, 39, 59, 68, 73
    disability 21
    as disincentive 93–4
    passive 66–7, 83, 89
    unemployment 19, 61, 66, 68–9
income tax 31, 32, *32*, 93, 95
    corporate 32
    and EU tax harmonization 95
    negative (tax credits) 58
income transfer payments 19, 22, 56, 58, 59
Indigenous and Tribal Peoples Convention, 1989
    (No. 169) 27

industrial relations
    Cooperation Agreement (1989) 80
    principles of 47–9
    *see also* collective bargaining; trade unions
inflation 31, 79
information, access to 51
information technology use 35
injuries
    fatal occupational 18
    non-fatal 18
institutions
    importance of 44–5, 95–6
    labour market 65
insurance, unemployment 19, 89
interest rates 95
International Labour Organization (ILO) xi, 5
    Committee on Freedom of Association 27–8
    Conventions 27, 40
    Decent Work paradigm vi, xi, 3
    Declaration on Fundamental Principles and
        Rights at Work (1998) v
    Working Party on the Social Dimension of
        Globalization v-vi
Internet use 35
investment
    inward 60
    by pension funds 61
Ireland xi, 8, 11, 28
    prosperity 30, 31
Italy 58, 69
    GDP per capita **75**

Japan 18, 70, 73, 77
    GDP per capita **75**
    public social security expenditure 22, *23*, 58
    unemployment 8, *70*
    working hours *16*, 77
job security 73, 80, 83, 89
    *see also* employment

Korea, Republic of 77

Labour Administration Convention, 1978
    (No. 150) 27

labour costs 61, 78
    non-wage 78
Labour Court 53
labour force 43
    mobility 67–70
    *see also* labour force participation; labour
        supply
labour force participation
    benefits conditional upon 56, 61, 73–4
    gender equality 23–4, *24*, 63
    inflows 70, **71**
    rate 6, *12*, 38
Labour Inspection (Agriculture) Convention,
    1969 (No. 129) 27
Labour Inspection Convention, 1947 (No. 81) 27
labour market policies 60, 65–75, 83–4
    and ageing workforce 92
    expenditure on 66, 70, **71**, 84
    "flexicurity" 66–7, *67*, 89–90
    mobility 67–70
    participant inflows 70, **71**
    prospects for 72–5
    public intervention 74
    to reduce unemployment 88
    reforms (1993) 73
    vocational training 72
    *see also* employment; labour supply
labour market training 68, 72
labour productivity 30, **37**, 75, 91
    GDP per hour worked 30, **75**, 77, 81
    GDP per person employed 30, 41, 77
    growth 77, 92–3
labour standards, international 27–8, 40
Labour Statistics Convention, 1985 (No. 160) 27
labour supply
    effect of EU enlargement on 94
    measures to maintain 87–8
    potential shortages 73–4, 78, 79–80
    and taxation 93–4
legislation
    and implementation of EU Directives 54, 94
    limited use of 27, 40, 46, 53–4
life expectancy 35, **37**, 41, 92

life, quality of 60, 77, 84
    satisfaction indicators 41–2
literacy 60
living standards 35, 41
long-term unemployment 8, *14*, 39, 69, 90
Luxembourg 8, 31
    EU Jobs Summit (1997) 3

macroeconomics
    expansionary policies 74, 78–9, 85
    imbalances 36, 38
    interaction with microeconomic policy 75–80
    and wage negotiations 53
    *see also* economic growth; economic
    performance indicators
manufacturing 77
    wages 10, *17*
marginalized workers 68
maternity
    benefits 56
    leave 21
means testing 57
men
    labour force participation 6, 23, *24*
    unemployment rate 8
mental illness 56
Minimum Age Convention, 1973 (No. 138) 27
minimum wages 11, 18, 39, 84
monetary policy 79, 95
mortgage interest rates 95

National Institute of Occupational Health 55
natural resources 41, 81
"negotiated economy" 47
Netherlands xi, 6, 9, 70
    employment rate **76**
    GDP per capita **75**
    part-time employment 7, *13*
    social expenditure 21, 58
    unemployment 8, *14*
    wages 18, 26, 64, 90
    working hours 10, *16*
networks 47

night work 10
Nordic Council of Ministers 91
Norway 9, 30, 31
    employment rate 6, *12*, 76, 88
    and EU 44
    GDP per capita **75**
    unemployment 8, 9, *14*
    work organization 28, 80
    working hours 10, *16*
notice, and severance pay 19–20

Occupational Health Service 55
occupational safety and health 18–19, 39, 91
    policies 54–6
Occupational Safety and Health (Construction)
    Convention, 1988 (No. 167) 27
Occupational Safety and Health Convention,
    1981 (No. 155) 27
Occupational Safety and Health (Dock Work)
    Convention, 1979 (No. 152) 27
occupational segregation, horizontal gender
    24–6, *25*, 40, 64–5
older workers
    employment rate 7, 77
    pensions 20, 21, 56
    and working conditions 91, 92, 94
Organisation for Economic Co-operation and
    Development (OECD) 5
    collective bargaining *29*
    economic and social indicators 30-32, *34*,
        38, 41
    education and training 9, *15*
    employment rate 6, 7, *12, 13*
    gender equality 23
    labour force participation rate *12*
    social security 19-22, *23*
    trade unions 28, *29*
    unemployment and inactivity 8, 9, *14, 15*
    wages and income 10, 11, *16*, 18

parental leave 21, 63, 64
parliament, women in 25
part-time employment 7, *13*
    EU Directive on 54

pensions
    labour market (income-based) 20
    private 20
    public old-age 20, 56
    semi-retirement 21, 56
    supplementary 20
police 77
politics, spirit of compromise 82
population 43
    demographic trends 79–80, 87, 92
    *see also* older workers; women
Portugal 8, 19, 26
poverty
    among jobless households 18
    effect of social transfers on 60
    relative 18, 40, 82, 84
price stability **37**, 48
private sector
    gender wage gap *26*, 65
    wage bargaining 51
prosperity 84
    GDP per capita 30–1
public expenditure
    on education and training 9, 77
    social security 22, *23*, 57–9, *59*
public health 56, 92
    *see also* occupational safety and health
public sector 45, 65, 83
    gender wage gap *26*, 52, 65
    wage bargaining 51
    women's employment 64

recession (1987-93) 36, 44
rehabilitation 56
retirement age 88, 92
    *see also* early retirement
Right to Organise and Collective Bargaining
    Convention, 1949 (No. 98) 27

safety, personal 60
Sector Safety Councils 55
self-employed, benefits 21
severance pay 19–20

shift work 10
sickness benefits 21, 56, 89
skills 60, 72, 91
    *see also* vocational training
small and medium-sized enterprises (SMEs) 45,
    46, 77, 81
social assistance (cash welfare benefits) 21–2,
    56, 77, 89
social cohesion 45, 82
social dialogue 29, 46, 80, 95–6
    *see also* collective bargaining; trade unions
social exclusion 56
social participation 40, 43, 45, 82
social protection 19–23, **20**, *23*, 74, 82
    effects of 59–62, 77–8
    indicators **34**, **37**, 38
    policy 56–62
    tax-financed 61–2, 93
social security expenditure
    public 22, *23*, 57–9, *59*
    voluntary private 57, 58, *59*, 62
Spain 10, 18, 28, 35
    employment rate **76**
    labour mobility 67–8
    social security 19, 59
State
    as facilitator 47, 48
    limited intervention 46, 47
    politics 82
    *see also* legislation
Statistics Denmark 5
stress, work-related 39, 91
strikes, rate 29–30
students, benefits 56
subsidiarity, principle of 57
subsidies 56
Sunday work 10
Sweden
    business regulations 35
    collective bargaining *29*, 50
    economic and social indicators 30, 35, **37**,
        **75**, 77
    education and training 9, *15*

employment rate 6, *12*, **76**, 77, 88
  and EU 44
  gender equality 26, 27, 63–4
  Good Work concept 81
  Internet use 35
  labour costs 61
  labour market expenditure 70
  social security 19, 21, 22, *23*, 57, 58
  taxation 31, 32, 33
  trade unions 28, *29*
  unemployment and inactivity 9, *15*, 19, 69
  wages and income 11, 51, **52**
  work organization 10, 80
  working hours *16*
Swedish National Board for Industrial and Technical Development 80
Switzerland 19, 31, 90

taxation 31–3, *32*, 41, 61, 62
  consumption taxes 33, 58
  EU harmonization policy 95
  and incentive to work 93
  individual 63
  and labour supply 93–4
  social security contributions 32, *32*
  of social transfers 58
  Whitsun Agreement reforms 93
  *see also* income tax
temporary workers 68
trade, facilitated 60
trade unions 49, 85
  membership density rate 28, *29*, 47
  pension fund management 61
  September Compromise (1899) 49–50
  and work organization 80–1
training 9, 39, 68
  craft 81
  vocational 41, 49, 72
Tripartite Consultation Convention, 1976 (No. 144) 27
Tripartite Statistics Committee 51
trust, in trade unions 28–9

unemployment
  duration 68
  frictional 90
  job rotation scheme 66, 90
  long-term 8, *14*, 39, 69, 90
  and low-employability groups 88
  marginalized workers 68
  potential structural 69
  structural 69
  volatility of 69–70
  *see also* labour market policies
unemployment benefits (protection) 19, 56, 60–1, 83
  income replacement rates 19, 61, 66, 68–9
  trade union administration 28
unemployment rates 8, *14*, **37**, *38*, 39, 73
  comparative *70*
  youth 8, *14*, 76
United Kingdom 9, 18
  employment rate **76**
  GDP per capita **75**
  income distribution 11, 26
  part-time employment *13*
  public social security expenditure 21, 58
United Nations Development Programme (UNDP)
  Human Development Index 41
  *Human Development Report* 84
United States 5, 28, 35, 59
  economic and social indicators 31, 33, **34**, **37**
  education *15*
  employment rate 6, 7, *12*, *13*, **76**, 77
  GDP per capita 75, **75**
  job insecurity 73
  labour costs 61
  labour market 68, 70
  labour productivity 30, 77
  private social security expenditure 62
  public social security expenditure 22, *23*, 57, 58, *59*
  social dialogue *29*
  taxation 31, 32, *32*, 33
  unemployment 8, *14*, *15*, 69, *70*, 90

wages and income 11, *17*, 18
    working hours 10, *16*, 77, 84
Universal Declaration of Human Rights 46
universalism, of welfare model 56

vocational education and training 41, 49, 72
Vocational Education and Training Act (2000) 72
Vocational Rehabilitation and Employment
    (Disabled Persons) Convention, 1983
    (No. 159) 27

wage inflation 90
wage negotiations 48, 50–3
    indexation 48
    and mortgage interest rates 95
wage restraint 52–3, 78, 79
wages
    distribution 11, 18, 83
    gender gap 26, *26*, 91
    hourly earnings 10–11, *17*, 51, **52**
    level and growth 10–11, *17*
    minimum 11, 18, 39, 84
    nominal 52–3
    real 11, **52**
welfare *see* benefits; social protection
welfare models 62–4
women
    in administration 24–5
    education 23, 64
    employment rate 6, 24, 62, 76, 83
    as entrepreneurs 26, 40, 91
    inactivity rate *15*
    labour force participation 6, 23–4, *24*, 63
    occupational segregation 24–5, *25*, *26*,
        40, 64–5

part-time employment 7, *13*
    unemployment rate 8, *14*, 39
    wage gap 26, *26*, 52, 65
    *see also* gender equality
work organization, flexible 80–1
worker participation 30, 54, 55, 91
workers
    employees' social security contributions 22
    influence over working conditions 30, 54, 55
    older 7, 77, 91, 92, 94
    temporary 68
working conditions 41, 91
    changing 39
    and older workers 91, 92, 94
    workers' influence over 30, 54, 55
    workplace design 81
    *see also* occupational safety and health
Working Environment Act (1975) 55
Working Environment Appeal Board 55
Working Environment Authority 55
Working Environment Council 55
working hours 10, *16*, 39, 75–6, 84
    annual 10, *16*, 77
    collective preference for short 77, 84
    and taxation rates 94
World Summit for Social Development v, vi, xi
Worst Forms of Child Labour Convention, 1999
    (No. 182) 27

young people
    employment rate 6, 76
    training 9
    unemployment rate 8, *14*, 76